MW00579147

Helen Duncan

The Two Worlds of Helen Duncan

by

Gena Brealey

with Kay Hunter

First Published by Regency Press 1985
ISBN 0-7212073-0-8

Re-published 2008
by
Saturday Night Press Publications
York, England
for contact use
snppbooks@gmail.com

ISBN 978-0-9557050-3-8

Printed by
Lightning Source
www.lightningsource.com

Cover illustration by Douglas Cameron

Foreword

On 26th October, 1956, the police interrupted a séance held in the Nottingham home of a respectable chiropodist.

Much has been written of the medium concerned. She has been described as one of the most controversial physical mediums - a martyr for Spiritualism.

In this biography I have told the true story of this remarkable woman. Her many gifts of clairvoyance, clairaudience and precognition have all been overshadowed by the publicity relating to the physical, or materialisation side of her mediumship.

Nothing has been written of her unselfish love for humanity, her devotion to her husband and family, her personal and private joys and tragedies, her physical and emotional suffering. The real truth has never been told.

Thirty-six days after the police intervened at the Nottingham séance, the medium was dead. Her name was Helen Duncan. She was my mother.

Gena Brealey

Acknowledgements

I would like to give grateful thanks to Kathleen Kirby of Toddington for her help and her unceasing conviction that I should tell Helen's story. Also to my husband and family for their support as I re-lived the heartache of the 1933 and 1944 trials and Helen's tragic death in 1956.

My sincere thanks to Kay Hunter for her research into Maurice Barbanell's account of the 1944 trial and for making it possible for the true story of Helen Duncan to be told.

Gena Brealey, 1985.
Sandyford, Stoke-on-Trent.

Publisher's Note on the authors

Gena Brealey was reunited with her mother, Helen, in 1986.

Kay Hunter has written books on such diverse subjects as Spiritualism and Theatre. Originally training as a teacher of music and drama she left that for a career in journalism and her association with the Spiritualist newspaper Psychic News extends over 30 years.

Her early books included 'Living Image' with Coral Polge and 'A Dance with Life' with dancer John Gilpin. Her eighth and latest book 'Ballet in the Blitz', published in 2008, is the record of a wartime ballet company.

Contents

1	The Beginning of the End	9
2	Warnings in Edinburgh	14
3	Childhood	17
4	Growing up	24
5	Henry's Experience	27
6	Discovering Love	32
7	Marriage - The Early Days	37
8	Developing the Gift	39
9	Trials and Tribulations	47
10	Helping the Serving	54
11	The Struggles for Perfection	59
12	Two Kinds of Test	69
13	The Working Medium	76
14	Accusations of Fraud	85
15	On Trial	90
16	The Good Years	104
17	Warnings of War	110
18	War and Witchcraft	113
19	The Scales of Justice	122
20	Coming Home	129
21	Back on the Treadmill	140
22	The End of the Beginning	155

Part II	**Due process of the Law**	161
1.	"Though justice be thy plea, consider this,-"	163
2.	"I charge you by the law,"	189
3.	"Take then thy bond,"	210
4.	"There is no power in Venice can alter a decree"	220
5.	"Earthly power doth then show"	232
6.	"Nothing but the plenty."	241
7	"You take my life,"	248

Chapter 1

The Beginning of the End

As Spiritualist medium Helen Duncan made her way
upstairs to the séance room in the home of a Nottingham
chiropodist on 26th October, 1956, she heard clairaudiently
the word "police".

Taking it to mean that friends from Nottingham
Constabulary would be attending the séance, she cheerfully
proceeded up the stairs towards the séance room, which had
been prepared earlier in the day. Two women quite
unknown to the medium had been asked to observe her
completely disrobe and re-dress herself only in the simple
black robe she wore during materialisation séances. The
practice of having two independent witnesses inspect her
clothes and remain with her until the time of the séance
had been carried out at her own request ever since her
controversial trial in Edinburgh in 1933. She wished to give
no opportunity for accusations of fraudulent mediumship
and was meticulous in her honest, pre-séance preparations.

Her two witnesses accompanied her up the stairs in the
Nottingham house to the well-lit room where chairs had
been placed in a half circle. One corner of the room had
been curtained off to form a "cabinet" for the medium. This
corner contained one straight-backed dining chair. The
windows were blacked out and the red light, which would

be turned on when the sitting began, had been so placed that it shone on the cabinet where Helen Duncan would be seated and from where any materialised spirit forms would appear.

Before taking her seat, Helen asked her two witnesses if they would please tell the other sitters what they had observed as she prepared for the séance. One of the two women spoke on behalf of both of them, telling those present that they had examined one black dress, black knickers and one pair of black court shoes. The medium had undressed and stood completely naked before re-dressing in the garments already examined and handed back to her.

"I also looked through Mrs Duncan's hair and she was not concealing anything," stated the spokeswoman. The other witness nodded in agreement. Helen then took her seat in the cabinet. The normal white room light was switched off and the red light switched on. Within a minute or two, as their eyes became accustomed to the change of light, everyone could clearly see each other and the corner where Helen Duncan was now sitting entranced. As was the custom, the sitters were asked to sing the 23rd Psalm and the curtain was closed over the cabinet. By the end of the first verse the voice of Helen's spirit control, 'Albert', was heard to say, "Good Evening."

At the first sound of Albert's voice, in the words of Helen's friend Mrs Gert Hamilton, "All hell broke loose."

There was a bright flash of light, a sudden banging on doors and a man's voice shouted, "Police!" Two bodies seemed almost to fly through the air towards the cabinet in an attempt to get to it quickly. Gert also rushed forward to help her friend, for she knew of the danger which could befall the medium through sudden light or touch without permission of the Control.

Gert was violently pushed aside and, as the room was

flooded with light, she saw a woman bending over Helen saying, "I have her."

Slumped forward, with a man's hands holding her shoulders, Helen lay perfectly still, her face a sickening grey colour.

"Oh God," thought Gert. "She's dead." But again the voice of Albert spoke saying, "It's all right, Mrs Hamilton."

The two men who had rushed forward towards Helen then told Gert that they were police officers and if she did not get out of the way she would be charged with obstructing the police in the execution of their duty. Gert was not concerned for herself at that moment, but was desperately anxious about Helen's condition.

"Can you not see the woman is dying?" she replied frantically. As she received neither answer nor reaction to her remark she pleaded that at least a doctor might be called.

The two officers said nothing, but carried the unconscious Helen out of the séance room into a bedroom across the hallway. A policewoman remained in the bedroom, but Gert Hamilton was refused permission to stay with her friend.

While all this was going on, other police officers had entered the house by the downstairs back entrance. There seemed to be police everywhere, as if they had come to disperse a mob of rowdies,

Instead of which they had invaded the home of a respectable chiropodist, where a few interested people had gathered together to witness psychic phenomena. Eventually order was restored and the police took statements from the sitters before they were allowed to leave the house. Gert was shown into a room where statements were being taken and again she demanded that a doctor be called to Mrs Duncan.

"Please be quiet and answer my questions," was the only

response she received from the officer is charge.

"What are you to Mrs Duncan?" he asked.

"I am her friend," replied Gert.

"Are you her accomplice?"

"Accomplice in what?"

"In this fraud," said the police officer. "Now tell us where you have hidden the masks and cloth."

"I don't know what you are taking about," said Gert. "I have hidden nothing. I have been with one of your police-women all this time and I want a doctor for my friend - now. She is a very sick woman."

Gert turned to leave the room and as she reached the door she was told to call a doctor. She asked the owners of the house for a telephone directory. To the day of her death Gert could never remember the name of the doctor she telephoned but she was able to persuade him to come at once.

While waiting for him to arrive, Gert went to the bedroom where she and Helen had been sleeping during their stay in the house. She discovered that all their suitcases had been thoroughly searched and their clothing thrown back in great disorder. The front door bell rang and as she hurried out of the bedroom down the stairs she saw a man being admitted by a policeman. It was the doctor, who was taken by the officer in charge to the room where Helen was being held. As they went into the room the policeman was explaining his version of what had happened and why the police were there.

It did not require an expert to see just how ill the woman was, who was lying on the bed. As the doctor checked her pulse and heartbeat he gravely shook his head.

"Well, what do you want me to do?" he asked.

"I want you to examine her vagina and anus for masks and cloth which she used to conjure ghosts," was the reply. "Then I can remove her."

"What!" said the doctor. "Good God man, do you realise this woman is in deep shock - a diabetic with a heart condition, who could die if you move her? I'll be no part of this."

He gave Helen an injection of insulin to counteract the shock and make her more comfortable. Gert was then allowed in to see her friend and immediately asked the doctor how she was.

"Very ill, very ill indeed," he answered quietly. "I can do no more, I'm sorry." He turned and left the room.

As soon as Gert was left alone with Helen she drew a chair up to the bedside and sat holding her hand, praying she would pull through. She spent what little remained of the night sitting by Helen's bed. The next day the police gave permission for them to leave Nottingham and return to their respective homes. Knowing that Helen was unfit to travel, Gert asked the chiropodist if they could possibly stay another night, which was gladly agreed to. Gert prayed that Helen would be well enough for them to catch a train to Edinburgh on the Friday morning.

Chapter 2

Warnings in Edinburgh

At the same time as the drama in Nottingham, strange phenomena were also taking place in the Duncan home in Rankellor Street, Edinburgh.

Mr Henry Duncan, Helen's husband, awoke in the early hours of Friday morning to see his wife standing at the foot of the bed. His first thought was that she had come home earlier than expected, as she was still wearing her coat. He was about to ask why, when he noticed that she was very pale and was crying.

"What's wrong, lass?" he asked.

"I was going to leave you, but I couldn't," came the quiet answer.

As she moved towards Henry it was as though she glided forward. He put his hand out to take hers and as he did so, she vanished. Realising that something was seriously wrong where Helen was concerned, Henry rose and dressed. As he did so it crossed his mind for some reason that it would be two hours before the post arrived. After making himself some tea and pondering over his experience, he decided to take a walk and pick up the early morning paper.

The time seemed to pass slowly until their youngest daughter Gena arrived, as she did each day at nine. Gena always went to her parents' home daily to see if they wanted any shopping and to do small household chores to help them. She always tried to go early when her mother was away so that she could satisfy herself that her father was all right. Gena noticed her father's agitation as soon as she went in the door. He would lift the paper to read, then put it down again without even glancing at it.

"Has anything happened, Dad?" she asked.

"Yes and no," was his reply. "Oh dear, I don't know what to think."

Gena said nothing, knowing that if she waited he would tell her more, which he did. He related what had happened in the early hours and it seemed to her that by recounting his experience he was examining the occurrence more for his own benefit than for any explanation for her.

"Try not to worry, Dad," she said. "Maybe the post will bring some news."

No more was said, as both father and daughter had their own thoughts. The silence was broken by the shrill sound of the doorbell. Gena hurried to answer it and as the door opened she gasped at the sight of a telegraph boy standing there.

"Duncan?" he asked.

Not trusting herself to speak, she nodded and took the telegram, returning to her father with her heart in her mouth. As he quickly tore open the envelope and read the telegram he seemed to wilt before her. He sat down, looked at her with tearful eyes and held out the piece of paper towards her. "Read," he said.

Gena took it and read: "HELEN SERIOUSLY ILL. POLICE INTERRUPTED SÉANCE. BRINGING HELEN HOME. EXPLAIN ON ARRIVAL. - GERT."

Gena and her father looked at each other. No words were

needed to tell what they thought or felt. This could be the end for a woman who was a wonderful wife and mother and the most controversial medium this country was to know.

This portent was to be fulfilled. Thirty-six days later, Helen was to leave her Henry for the greater call of her Maker.

Chapter 3

Childhood

Victoria Helen McCrae MacFarlane was born on 25th November, 1895, the third child of Archibald MacFarlane and his wife Isabella.

The couple were from a line of hard-working, God-fearing people and Archibald was a master builder and slater by trade.

Within a few weeks of her birth, as was the usual custom Helen was baptised into the Scottish Presbyterian Church. She slept through most of the service, only waking for the actual naming and Blessing. As the minister made the sign of the cross with holy water, she opened her beautiful large brown eyes, then promptly went back to sleep.

The first seven years of Helen's life were no different from those of her brothers and sisters, learning, playing and growing in the clear healthy Scottish air. Always rather plump, her beauty lay in her large deep brown eyes, unusual blue-black hair and wonderful personality.

It was at this tender age that she began to show signs of being psychic, indications which were always met with rebuff. Once when her mother was baking, Helen, who had been quietly watching, suddenly asked, "Who is Johnny?"

"Why?" asked her mother.

"Oh, because he's here and saying he's not dead. I'm to tell you to tell his mother he is happy."

Greatly disturbed, her mother told Helen not to say things like that. Johnny had been killed before she was born, she said and if she continued to say things like that, people would say she was a witch and put her in prison. (Little was this woman to know that forty years later her prophesy was to come true.)

Helen, chastened, went out into the back garden and sat on the step, tears falling down her cheeks. She just did not understand why her mother was so angry, or why she had not believed her. She always told the truth, even when it meant being punished for doing wrong.

Why could they not see Johnny? He was like them-flesh and blood and in a soldier's uniform. A new wave of sobbing overcame her as she repeated to herself, "I did see him! I did, I did!"

Then she heard a voice saying, "Yes, you did see him. One day they will believe."

A feeling of calm swept over her and suddenly she was a child again, smiling as she got up from the stone step to skip happily away to play.

Always a sensitive child, Helen was slowly beginning to realise she was different from her friends. Sometimes she would predict to them things that would happen in the near future, or sometimes tell them of things which had happened to them in the past, which she could not possibly know about. At other times she would warn them to take care, her caution always proving well-founded. There was the incident of the village doctor who had gone missing in a blinding snowstorm. The local people, fearing he had had a serious accident, organised a search party. Hearing her parents discussing this, Helen said, "Don't worry. He's not far from here. They'll find him." As her father and mother looked at her, Helen realised she had again done what her mother had warned her not to do, so she quickly went out of the room.

Within a matter of hours, a neighbour came to tell the MacFarlanes that the doctor had been found close by. His car had gone into a snowdrift just a few miles away. Neither parent mentioned this outcome to Helen, but she knew they had earmarked the incident as another "odd thing" about her.

In the summer Helen would go swimming with her brother Peter in a pond not far from the village. All the local children had been warned of the danger of swimming there, as the pond had been used as a dump for all kinds of rubbish. Like all youngsters who thrive on the added thrill of danger, the children would secretly slip across the fields to their favourite spot. No matter what precautions they took in order not to be seen, their mother would always know when they had been swimming. For some time this puzzled Helen, until one night, on going downstairs for a glass of water, she overheard her mother telling her father of the look of bewilderment on Helen's face when confronted with the accusation that she had been swimming.

Helen's heart beat faster. Now she was going to learn the answer.

"How did you know she'd been swimming?" queried her father.

"Well," her mother replied, "Helen's petticoat should fasten down the back, but when she has to put it on herself she can only fasten it down the front."

So that was it. Never again will I be caught, thought Helen. After that she was careful to see that Peter always helped her with her petticoat, ensuring it was correctly fastened down the back!

As she grew and learned, Helen became more careful to keep her psychic feelings to herself, but sometimes they just came out.

At school one day the teacher informed the children that he was giving out the slates for a history test. Poor Helen, never a good scholar, could not understand the feeling of strange excitement as she looked at the questions on the blackboard. She clutched her slate to her chest and tried to think of something stirring at the back of her mind. What was it? Oh yes, the minister had been talking about Jesus and she remembered him saying, "Ask and you will receive." She prayed that she would remember and get the test right.

After what seemed a long time, but was actually only a few moments, Helen replaced the slate on her desk, still with nothing resembling answers in her head. As she looked down at her slate she was amazed to see that all the questions had been answered. Not realising how this had happened, but accepting the gift with childish simplicity, she sat back and folded her arms so that the teacher, Mr Cummings, would know she had finished. He came to her desk and lifted her slate. Knowing Helen's usual standard, he could not be blamed for asking where the book was.

"What book?" asked Helen dumbfounded.

"The book you got the answers from," he replied firmly.

"I have no book," stated Helen.

"I will overlook this, Helen," said Mr Cummings quietly, "If you will give me the book, or any paper on which you have the answers written."

"I have no book or paper," she protested. "I only held the slate to me and the answers were there."

"I have heard some stories in my time, but this takes some beating," said Mr Cummings angrily. "I'll soon knock that nonsense out of you!"

He walked to his desk and took up the cane, approaching Helen with it in a threatening manner.

Shaking, but also angry, Helen lifted the inkwell out of

her desk and suddenly let fly at the danger approaching her. As the inkwells had been newly filled for writing practice, the damage to Mr Cummings' clothes was considerable. However, Helen did not wait to see where her missile landed. She fled from the classroom as soon as the inkwell had left her hand. Running as fast her plump legs would carry her, which was as far as the turning into Bridge Street, she rested to recover her breath. Still gasping, but wanting the comfort of home, she ran again down the lane to Cherry Cottage.

Bursting in through the kitchen door, she poured out to her mother in what seemed like one breath, "I've run away from school and I'm not going back. I didn't have a book. I didn't have a book, the answers were just there!"

She broke into racking, shaking sobs and her shocked mother put her arms around her. "Sit down, girl," she said. "Nothing is that bad. I'm sure we can sort it out between us."

It seemed an age before Helen could conquer the waves of misery engulfing her. She felt she was being drowned in something she could not understand, but at last she managed to blurt out the story of how she finished the test first and was accused of cheating. "But I didn't cheat," she protested. "I only....."

She stopped before telling her mother about the answers on the slate. All too often she had been told by her mother not to talk about "those stories" of hers.

"Yes, Helen? You only what?" asked her mother.

"I only finished first," came the lame answer.

"Very well, if that's the truth your father will deal with it later."

"Well, it is the truth, but not all," said Helen, "I'm sorry, but I threw the inkwell with ink in it at Mr Cummings."

"Oh dear, your temper will get you into very serious

trouble," warned her mother. "Let's hope no damage was done and that your father can sort it out."

Isabella MacFarlane was a very gentle person, but understood her daughter's sudden outbursts of temper. She was very much like her father, especially if wrongly accused.

After hearing the story from his wife and having closely questioned Helen, Archie MacFarlane went to see the teacher. Both men were old friends, on Christian name terms, so he was greeted warmly by Cummings.

"Do come in, Archie. I thought you would come."

"Now what's all this about, William?" asked Archie.

"Sit down, man, and have a drink," replied Mr Cummings. "I'll explain what happened."

Handing the worried father a glass of whisky, the teacher gave his account of what had taken place at school that morning. His account was much the same as Helen's, but he added what Helen had not waited to see; the missile had found its mark and ink had spattered all down the front of his jacket.

"I'm so sorry William. I'll pay for it and I'll make sure that Helen apologises tomorrow," said her father, acutely embarrassed.

"Let's say no more about it, Archie. I'm probably just as much to blame for accusing the poor wee lass of cheating."

"Did she?" asked Archie.

"Certainly not to my knowledge," replied the teacher.

The men then discussed various village affairs and after a pleasant hour or so Archie rose to leave, promising to see his friend again soon.

Helen arrived at school next day with mixed feelings. She had certainly not cheated, yet in a way, in her own mind, she had. Were not the answers written down for her? Yet she had been prepared to take the credit for them, hadn't she? When the school bell rang she went straight in to wait at Mr Cummings' desk. She need not have worried. As the teacher entered the room he smiled at the troubled girl and the ice was broken.

"I'm sorry, sir," she murmured.

"It's all right, lass. I may have been hasty. Now go back to your seat."

Helen's classmates were not so quick to let the incident die. When they broke for lunch, the boy who sat next to Helen slipped at piece of paper into her hand which read:

> *Tiger Cummings in a rage,*
> *Like a monkey in a cage.*
> *When the ink went down his back*
> *He was like a jumping jack.*

All her life Helen was quick to anger, yet like a true Sagittarian, within minutes she would be sorry for her lack of control, but also true to her birth sign she had an innate sense of what was just. Nothing angered her more than being falsely accused; it did not only anger, but caused a deep hurt. She carried this trait for the whole of her life.

Chapter 4

Growing Up

Work was hard to come by in the small village of Callander. Those who could not find employment on farms or in service locally went into the towns. Helen and her parents discussed what she should do and eventually it was decided that she would go to Dundee to work in the jute mills. Initially she would live in a young women's hostel until she was used to being away from home.

Everything at first was strange and exciting. There was the adventure of work and making friends with the people she worked with. The hostel was completely different from home, with girls giggling and laughing and trying hard to appear more grown up and adult than they really were. While enjoying the company, it was not long before Helen began to miss her family. She took to going home at weekends and her parents were delighted to have their daughter home so often, but were unaware that in order to pay the train fares on her meagre wage, Helen often went without proper food.

About six months after Helen started work a new girl started at the mill and was assigned by the foreman to work with Helen. The two girls soon became firm friends and discovered they had much in common. Both liked dancing and country walks. Sometimes when the weather was cold, the ice on the old quarry, which the locals called Parmay Pond, was thick enough to skate on. Many happy hours were spent adding ice-skating to their activities.

Visits home to Callander became less frequent and in 1914, when war was declared, both girls volunteered for service in a munitions factory. Jane and Helen were sent for the requisite medical examination. Jean, a tiny dainty girl of six and a half stone, was passed as fully fit, while poor Helen, who tipped the scales at fifteen stone, was declared unfit for service. The medical examination revealed that she had tuberculosis of the left lung. She spent the next few months in the Sanatorium, where with regular meals, proper rest and fresh air, she made a remarkable recovery. However, her time spent in the sanatorium made a great impression upon her. She no longer wanted to work in the jute mills, but felt a great desire to help to care for others as she herself had been looked after.

In less than a year Helen secured a job as a Nursing Aid in the Dundee Royal Infirmary. She enjoyed the work and as there was no longer the worry about having regular meals or walking to work in the cold wet weather, her health continued to improve. Jean, who had frequently visited Helen in the sanatorium, now began to visit her in her room at the hospital when both girls had time off. One evening as they sat talking, Helen told Jean of a strange dream she had been having.

"I dreamt I was in France and could see this young soldier and felt that this was the man I would marry."

She explained to Jean that she had dreamt this three times. "But last night the young soldier was no longer standing in the trenches," she said. "I could see him in hospital, looking very ill. What do you think it means?"

Jean replied that she was probably thinking about the war and about her own stay in hospital. Also, as the local paper printed lists of the latest war wounded, it was probably all getting mixed up in her mind. But Helen was not convinced.

"You don't understand," she said. "That would not account for my feeling that the soldier was the man I'm going to marry."

The subject was then dropped and the girls went on to chatter about other things.

Chapter 5

Henry's Experience

A young soldier looked over the top of the trench where he stood ankle deep in mud. His eyes took in the now empty battlefield. Two days before, this same field had been the scene of bitter fighting between British and German forces, victory going to neither. Both sides had withdrawn to the safety of the dug-out trenches.

Henry, a Private in the Black Watch, was cold and tired after a long night's vigil on watch. His thoughts drifted to his home in Dundee, to his father William, his mother Annie, sisters Jean and Annie and the twins, Robert and Alec. He worried about his mother, who suffered from diabetes, but the last letter from home had been quite cheerful and reassuring. His father, a shipwright, had secured a job on the docks. Jean, a year older than himself, had left the jute mills and gone into a munitions factory . . The voice of the sergeant broke in on his thoughts.

"Anything to report, Private?"

"All quiet, Sergeant."

The two men had become friends after sharing many tight corners during their time on guard duty together. The young soldier was only seventeen and had been very frightened at the hell-hole of the trenches. As an old campaigner the sergeant would talk to him of his home and family, recognising his fear and trying to dispel it. Living as they were, in constant touch with death, it seemed only natural that the possibility of life after death was discussed. Henry, the young soldier, was a firm believer in the survival of the spirit in everyone, also the communication which existed between spirit and loved ones still on the earth plain.

He told the sergeant of the time when his young brother, aged eight, had gone missing from home. After weeks of searching by police, family and friends, no trace was found of the little boy William, who had been named after his father. It was as though he had vanished into thin air. More from desperation than with any feeling of belief, the parents had gone to a Spiritualist meeting, where the medium had spoken to them.

"I feel this lady is very worried about a little boy," she said, coming to his mother. "I see water, I see ships. I feel I am somewhere in a harbour. Three weeks from now there will be news."

Greatly impressed, William went to the police the following day and told the policeman in charge of the search what he had been told by the medium.

"You surely don't expect me to have the docks dragged on the say-so of one of those quacks?" retorted the sergeant.

"Anything is worth a try," replied the heartbroken father.

"Very well, I'll get in touch with the force at the docks again and ask them to search," agreed the sergeant reluctantly.

Three weeks later the small body was dragged from the water. Little William had fallen between the quay and a boat which was in for repair. When the ship was moved upon completion of the repair, his body, which had been trapped, was released.

This had not been Henry's first experience of the supernatural. One evening, as he had climbed the stairs to his tenement home, he had smelled gas. He hurried into the house and asked his mother if she could also smell gas.

"No," she replied.

"I'll check again," said Henry. "It seems to be stronger on the stairs."

Going back to the front door, he saw a young woman washing her hands in the communal sink, which served two families on the landing. The girl seemed to be crying. Just as he was about to ask her if she could smell gas, she vanished. Henry closed the door, ran back to his mother and told her what he had seen.

"Don't be silly, laddie. It must have been a trick of the light," said his mother.

The boy knew differently, but he let the incident pass, saying nothing more. Not long afterwards Henry sat talking to his father when his father said suddenly, "I don't like this house. When I come up the stairs I feel so depressed. Then when I come into our flat I want to throw things about. I don't understand it."

"Can I tell you something, Dad?" said Henry. And without waiting for an answer he told his father about the smell of gas and the young woman crying, then vanishing. He then went on to tell him about a strange dream which kept recurring. A big man would be standing in the corner of his room, looking at him menacingly. As the man started to come towards him, Henry would awake, sweating with the feeling that the man was about to strangle him.

"But the strange thing is, Dad, I don't feel as if it's me lying in the bed. Does that make sense?" asked the boy.

His father did not answer him immediately. Then he looked at him and said ponderously, "I wonder.

"Wonder what, Dad?"

"Never mind. I'll make a few enquiries," said his father.

William did make enquiries and the first thing he discovered was that the flat had been empty for over a year when he and his family moved in. The rent was low and the flat was in good repair, so why had it been empty for so long? Try as he might, he could find nobody who could or would tell him. Finally, he went directly to the landlord and asked him about the previous tenants. He was told that the couple who had lived there had met with a tragic end. The husband had been a drunkard and a bully and had taken to beating his wife. The poor woman had somehow managed to fit a tube from the gas pipe on the landing to the keyhole in her room and had ended her misery by taking her own life. Within a few weeks the husband had hanged himself. After revealing all this, the landlord then offered to find William and his family another place to live.

Henry thought of all these things often in the grim surroundings of France during the war.

Eventually orders came to move back twelve miles from the Front. The men were exhausted after many weeks in the bitter fighting of the front lines and were to be relieved for a well earned rest. As they started the march back to base camp, Henry felt every bone and joint in his body ache. After a few miles he was hardly able to walk and was sweating profusely. He tried to keep marching, but at last he fell. He was vaguely aware of hands lifting him and a voice saying, "Not far now, son. You'll make it."

Henry slowly became conscious of smells of disinfectant, the noises of men moaning and the clink of glass. Opening his eyes, he saw a nurse standing by his bed, writing on a small board.

"I see you're back with us," she said, smiling.

"How long have I been here?" asked Henry.

"A week. You have rheumatic fever. The doctor will be round soon and will talk to you."

After straightening the bed, the nurse moved on to the next.

As he looked around Henry saw men with broken limbs, bandaged heads, some had arms or legs missing and the poor soul next to him had lost both legs. He closed his eyes and silently thanked God that at least he was whole.

"Not disturbing you, am I?" said a voice.

Opening his eyes, Henry saw a handsome young man smiling down at him. He tried to sit up and said, "Sorry sir, I was dreaming."

The young doctor put his hand on his shoulder and told him to stay as he was. He went on to explain that the rheumatic fever had badly damaged a valve of his heart and that it would take him a while before he was up and about. As the doctor moved on to the next patient he told Henry that as soon as he was strong enough he would be shipped home to recover fully.

Drifting into sleep again, Henry once more saw the face of a young girl. He could hear himself saying, "What's your name?" The face smiled and vanished. This was now a regular pattern of his illness. He had seen this face often; it was one of the last things he was aware of before he fell on the march. At that time she had spoken and her words were, "You will be all right." Then the blackness had engulfed him.

Now Henry muttered, "I like you," before he fell into a deep, health-restoring sleep.

Chapter 6

Discovering Love

Having been invalided home to a military hospital in Edinburgh, Henry soon made good progress towards full strength. After a while he was allowed home at weekends.

One weekend he arrived home to find his mother preparing tea and laying the table in the parlour.

"Visitors?" he asked.

"Yes. Jean is bringing a friend to tea."

"Do I know her?" said Henry.

"No," replied his mother. "Even I don't know her. It's strange that Jean has been friends with this girl for over two years, but this is the first time she's brought her home."

At four o'clock Jean arrived with her friend. As she turned to introduce Helen to her mother she noticed that Henry and Helen were staring at each other. Saying a kind Hello, Jean's mother left to bring in the tea. Breaking the silence that followed, Henry said, "So we meet at last."

The young couple never spoke to each other again until after tea. When Helen had to go because she was on duty at eight, Henry rose and asked if he could walk her back. As they walked along the Ferry Road, Henry asked why she had never been to the house before.

"Just one of those things," replied Helen. "Jean and I

used to meet in town when we first became friends, then I was nine months in a sanatorium with a spot on my lung. And of course, now I'm a Nursing Aid I only see Jean occasionally, as the hospital has been so busy. With this flu epidemic we have been working very hard."

By the time they reached the hospital gates Henry realised he was talking to a natural psychic and wondered to himself how well this gift could be developed. His thoughts were interrupted by Helen's voice.

"What are you thinking about, Henry?"

Turning to look her straight in the eye, Henry asked, "Do you know what a clairvoyant is?"

"No," answered Helen. "Is that what's wrong with you?"

"Good heavens, no," replied Henry, going on to explain what the word meant.

This naive assumption of Helen's was eventually to become a family joke, as was another some years later when she was a patient in Edinburgh Royal Infirmary. Each patient had a chart beside the bed and on Helen's was clearly printed, against 'Reason for Admittance', the word "Spiritualist".

During the 7 months which followed, the young couple spent many happy hours together. Realising theirs was a true and lasting love, Henry asked Helen to marry him. The shy reply came not as a simple Yes, as he expected, but she said, "I'm sure it has already been arranged in Heaven that we two will always be together."

Thinking of his experience in France when he had clairvoyantly seen this wonderful girl, he nodded and said, "I too believe that."

Deciding to marry as soon as they could find a suitable place to live, they began, every week, to buy the things they would need in their first home. Fortune was kind and a friend who lived in Edinburgh soon told them of a flat to let in Forrest Road. This was very near the statue of Greyfriars Bobby, the dog who, when his master died, lay beside the grave for fourteen years until he too was laid to rest, close by the grave he so lovingly guarded.

As the wedding preparations were under way, Helen took Henry to meet her family in Callander. It was important to her that the family she loved would in turn love and approve of the man she also loved. Mrs MacFarlane gave her daughter and her "intended" a warm welcome, but Henry later admitted that it seemed a very long day before Mr MacFarlane returned from work. Helen tried to make Henry relax by taking him for a walk around the village in which she had spent her childhood. She showed him where she used to play, the school and related the story of the slate, Mr Cummings and the inkwell. She took great pride in showing him the cottage her father had built. Victoria Cottage was named after Queen Victoria and led to an interesting family story. .

When Isabella MacFarlane was a child, her mother one day answered the door to a gentleman in Highland dress. He asked if the two ladies sitting in an open carriage just outside the house could come and take shelter from the rain. It was a wet and cold day and Helen's grandmother, always a warm-hearted and kindly person, said they would be very welcome to come in for a warming cup of tea. She left the man to bring in the ladies and hurried to make the tea from the already hot kettle on top of the kitchen range. Hearing another knock at the door, without stopping her preparations, she called, "Come away in, man, and bring your friends. Take a seat and warm yourselves by the fire. I'll no be a minute. Find yon towel by the door and dry yourselves while I pour."

A pleasant hour was spent talking to the ladies, whom

Helen's grandmother felt were high bred and "of the quality" as was said in those times. When they rose to continue their journey, the gentleman asked if Mrs Rattery had anything they could borrow to pin their dresses with, to prevent them from trailing in the mud on the path, which was becoming like a quagmire with the continuing rain. Pins were provided, but when the gentleman requested if he could borrow an umbrella to further save the ladies from the rain, Mrs Rattery was more hesitant.

"Well, I dinna ken. Ye see, I've only got one brolly and that ma man brought me when he went to Stirling."

Assuring her that the umbrella would be returned the next day, she agreed that it might be borrowed. The younger and taller of the two ladies pinned up the other lady's dress, then hurriedly pinned her own. Both ladies thanked Mrs Rattery for her kindness and hospitality.

The following day she was most upset when the promised return of the umbrella never came. However, a week later, when she had almost forgotten about her loss, a carriage again stopped outside the cottage. This time Mrs Rattery was already at the door, as she had heard the noise of the carriage drawing up. A man dressed in livery alighted and enquired as he approached, "Mrs Rattery?"

Nodding her head she whispered a surprised, "Yes?" all the while wondering who it could be. She was handed a box neatly wrapped and tied with string. Through the string was pushed an official looking brown envelope.

"What's this for?" she asked.

Standing smartly to attention, the man replied, "I am instructed by Her Most Gracious Majesty to give you this box and to thank you for your kindness and hospitality."

He then saluted, turned quickly and returned to the carriage, leaving a bemused and speechless Mrs Rattery standing on the doorstep. Regaining some of her senses and trying to control her emotion, she went into the house and put the box on the kitchen table. She took out the letter and read it. It was from the queen's lady-in-waiting, thanking her again for all she had done and also returning the umbrella. She looked at the signature and stamp. Quietly to herself she said, "So that's who it was and I didna bring oot ma best cheenie. Oh my! Archie will no forgive me!" Archie was Helen's grandfather. .

Henry found this story both amusing and interesting, but he was nevertheless glad to find that on returning to the cottage, Helen's father was home and the ordeal of meeting the bride's father could be met and dealt with. Archie MacFarlane was sad to lose his youngest daughter, but glad she had found such a good steady man as Henry Duncan.

Chapter 7

Marriage - Early Days

On 27th May, 1919, Henry Duncan and Helen MacFarlane were married and moved into their first home in Forrest Road, Edinburgh. Happy and enjoying getting their home together, it was a blow when their first Christmas together was marred by Helen's admission to hospital suffering from lobar pneumonia. She was extremely ill and unconscious for three days, during which time Henry sat by her bedside, leaving only when persuaded by hospital staff to go home to eat and wash.

At last Helen opened her eyes and upon seeing Henry sitting there she smiled and in a voice barely audible said, "I have something to tell you."

"Later my dear," replied Henry, gently stroking her hand.

Helen smiled and went into a normal sleep. The crisis was over. By visiting hour next day, she was so much better that she managed to brush and braid her hair. As Henry approached the bed he knew that she was excited, but was trying to keep herself under control. As he sat on the chair he had so recently vacated he said, "How are you lass?"

"Much better now you're here," came the quick response. Gripping her husband's hand, Helen said, "I've had very strange but wonderful experience."

"Tell me," smiled Henry.

"I remember you holding my hand, then slowly you vanished into a mist. Suddenly there was a man standing by my bed and putting out his hand to take mine, he asked me to go with him. I felt a bit apprehensive, but his voice was so compelling that I took his hand and arose. We came to a river and when I looked across at the other side it was so beautiful. Still holding hands we walked across, over the water. On reaching the other side I found myself alone. As I looked about me I could see flowers of every colour and grass a green I've never seen before. Suddenly to my right I saw a light. As I looked it became brighter and brighter until I had to shade my eyes. Then in the light a lectern appeared and on it lay an open book, as if someone had blotted it.

"Then I heard a man's voice calling my name. 'Yes,' I answered. As I watched and listened a hand with an out-stretched finger pointed to the book and a voice said, 'Helen, this is how your life has been.' Then the hand passed over the book and wiped it clean. The voice said, 'You will now return and do good and work for the service of others.' The light then went smaller and smaller until it completely vanished. Again the man who had taken me there appeared and said it was time to go. I looked across the water to the other side. It was all grey and dirty and I told him I didn't want to go back.

"Taking my hand he said I must, as there was so much work for me to do. So we started to cross and as we got near the side I saw a coffin..."

At this point Helen stopped talking and started to cry. Giving her hand a reassuring squeeze, Henry said, "It's all right, lass. Go on."

Sighing, Helen said, "On the coffin lid was a little brass plaque on which was inscribed:-Annie Maims Duncan. Died 8th March, 1928. I'm so sorry, Henry."

Nine years later, on 8th March, 1928, Henry's mother, Annie Maims Duncan, passed away from this side of life.

Chapter 8

Developing the Gift

Having joined the army when very young, Henry had no trade. He was offered an apprenticeship to a cabinet-maker and in order to secure his and his wife's future, accepted the opportunity. This meant returning to Dundee, where the business was, so the young couple left their first home and went back to Dundee.

Most evenings on the way home from work, Henry would buy little ornaments and trinkets - in fact, anything he could pick up cheaply. He was determined to do all he could to develop his wife's psychic gifts. The trinkets he could use to help develop the gift of psychometry. He would have Helen hold them in her hand and sense from them exactly where he had bought them. Soon she became quite good at this. She could even tell him how much he had paid for the article and whether he had managed to get it cheaper than the original asking price.

Reading and hearing of the many different types of psychic phenomena, Henry wished to investigate Helen's potential as a physical medium.

The first phenomenon happened by accident. One evening there was an electrical fault at the sub-station. The two children had been put to bed and a friend called Jim Murray had called to visit. He and Henry were in deep discussion about psychic matters and all three of them were sitting in candlelight. Helen, feeling ignored, leaned forward towards one of the candles and blew it out. By the light of the other candle, vapour from the extinguished candle could be seen clearly forming itself into the letters of the name "Williams". Both men were speechless at first, then started talking together. Henry would never accept phenomena without fully demanding to know how it was done. Turning to his wife he said, "What did you do?"

No answer came.

"I think she's entranced," said Jim.

"She's pretending to be asleep you mean," said Henry, relighting the candle which Helen had put out.

"Good evening, gentlemen. My name is Dr Williams."

Although the voice came from Helen's direction, it was independent of her vocal chords. Henry was the first to find his voice and loudly demanded that his wife stopped playing games, believing that she had somehow managed to throw her voice.

Again the man's voice answered. "I don't believe she can hear you, Duncan. I don't play games, I assure you. We have so much work to do we don't have time to play silly games as you do, bringing little gifts to Mrs Duncan to psychometrise. You would have been better employed sitting quietly one night a week and letting her develop the important gift in her field."

"What do you mean?" asked Henry.

"Surely you must know by now that your good lady is a physical medium and we would have you put aside one night a week at a specific time to develop the instrument. In order to develop, there have to be changes made in the body. To make this possible we need time to complete it. Will you do this, Duncan? I would also ask that you have two or three other friends join us, to help to give power for future phenomena. Will you do this for us?"

"Yes," answered Henry.

"Thank you. Before I go - Mr Murray, can I ask whether Mr or Mrs Duncan have been in your home?"

"No," replied Jim.

"You are sure of this?"

"Definitely."

"I want you both to watch Mrs Duncan, please."

The voice then told Helen to hold out her hand and as both men watched, a tie pin slowly began to appear in her hand. As it fully materialised the voice said, "You can take it now, Mr Murray. I think you will find it is yours, from a box in your bedroom. Good-night. God bless you and remember all I have said."

In their excitement at this unexpected séance, poor Helen was forgotten. It was not until she moaned a little and asked for a drink of water that the two men remembered her presence. They were examining the tie pin and verified that it was Jim's.

"I know it's mine," said Jim. "I accidentally stood on it and bent it.

Also, see where Frank, my brother, has scratched his initials on the back!"

Hearing Helen's request for a drink, Henry turned to her saying, "Are you all right, lass?"

"Yes," she murmured. "Please may I have a glass of water, I'm parched."

Thursday evening was the night chosen for the developing circle. This was the most convenient time for the brothers Jim and Frank Murray and another friend, Joe Sauter. Because of the sincerity of the sitters, development was fast and evidential. They soon witnessed proof of life after death and the survival of the spirit or as some people can better understand it, the survival of the soul after the physical body is no more.

In the beginning Doctor Williams, the "control", instructed them through direct voice of the procedure to be followed for the development of Materialisation, or Physical Phenomena. He explained that the time and place selected for the meetings must never be altered. As they had chosen the time for their communion with Spirit they must now abide by it. Also, they were never to accept anything at face value, but always question anyone claiming to come from the world of spirit, asking for evidence and proof which could be verified. In this way they would only receive the best of truth and knowledge. Some years and much heartache was to pass before any real materialisation evidence was to be experienced.

Henry and Helen had two children and then a third child was born - Henrietta. Sadly she was born with both arms and legs dislocated, which was attributed to the fact that Helen had developed Eclampsia, a toxaemic kidney disease. During labour she had suffered a convulsion resulting in the baby's injuries. Etta was a lovely child who adored her father. The family was told she would never be able to walk or use her limbs properly. It could have been as a result of the draughty old house or simply the mercy of Spirit but at the age of thirteen months little Etta passed. She was rushed to Dundee Royal Infirmary suffering from pneumonia but after one week passed into spirit.

Henry was devastated at the baby's death. He walked about for weeks as if in some kind of limbo, hardly eating or sleeping. Eventually he had a complete nervous break-down and a heart attack. Helen was pregnant with her fourth child and the birth came only four weeks after Etta's death. She too was extremely upset at the death of her little girl, but her grief was submerged in her anxiety about her husband's state of mind. On the day of his heart attack Helen was waiting for him to come home when she heard clairaudiently her name being called. The voice then said, "Henry. . . hurry."

Without pausing to think she called a neighbour and asked her to care for the children. She then ran to the cabinet-maker's shop, which by now was owned by Henry, but the door was locked.

"Please God, help me," she cried, panic-stricken.

As if in direct answer to her prayer, a policeman walked round the corner. He knew Helen and Henry.

"What's the matter, Mrs Duncan?" he asked.

"I don't know," said Helen, "But I must get into the shop. I feel my husband is in there and is ill."

The policeman was aware of the recent loss of their little girl and felt sorry for them. "I could break down the door if you want, lass," he offered.

"Yes, anything, but I must get in," replied Helen anxiously.

The policeman put his shoulder to the door and with a couple of good heaves, it gave way. Helen rushed in past him to the back workshop, where she found Henry slumped over a desk. He had been doing the account books when he had suffered a heart attack.

The policeman took charge and told Helen to call for an ambulance while he looked after Henry. Helen could never remember clearly what happened next, but she must have done what was needed. The next thing she was aware of was a grave-faced doctor, telling her that they had caught Henry just in time, but he was very ill. It was to be many months before he finally returned home to his family. After his stay in Dundee Hospital he was sent for further rest and treatment to the Veterans' Hospital near Aberdeen.

Alone with her children, Helen struggled to manage. Her fourth baby, another girl, was born and Helen named her Lilian. Life's cruelty had not yet finished with the Duncan family.

The eldest child, Isabella, was sent to stay with friends while Helen was having the baby. As the friends lived in a caravan, Helen was not too happy about Isabella going there, but with Henry in hospital and no one who could take both children, she had little choice. The aunt who took the younger girl felt unable to cope with both children.

When Lilian was two weeks old and just at the time when the other two children were due to return home, Helen had visitors. It was the two friends who were looking after Isabella. Just one look at their faces and Helen knew there was something dreadfully wrong. She was not prepared for the terrible news they had come to impart.

The little one had been asleep while the couple were outside, busy with their chores. Hearing her screaming, they had rushed in. To their horror they saw a ferret holding on to the child's face. When they managed to prise open the animal's jaws, they could hardly see the little face, which was a mass of blood. In a fever of shock and anxiety they wrapped little Isabella in towels and rushed her to the hospital.

The child's face had been terribly mutilated. The ferret had eaten the eyelid, eyeball and part of the bridge of the nose, injuries from which Isabella never mentally recovered. She changed completely from a lovely pleasant, natural child into a crying and argumentative whiner, causing friction in the family and always bitterly blaming her mother for what happened. Helen also blamed herself for what had happened to the child and carried a burden of self-hate throughout her life because of the tragedy. The friends with whom Isabella was staying at the time paid all hospital and doctor's bills. They were distraught, wanting to help in any way they could and even offering to adopt the little girl.

Helen knew this would have the worst possible effect on Isabella; so much had happened to her. First, her belief that she was being neglected when sent away while the baby was born, then her terrible accident which had left her so disfigured. It would have been impossible to inflict her with further imagined rejection by allowing her to leave home. The friends eventually emigrated to America and all contact with them was lost.

Although the circle had been discontinued because of Henry's illness, every Thursday the three men would visit Helen and the children. It was a great help to her to have such sincere friends. She was also grateful for their generosity; they were always bringing little gifts for the children and also food and clothes because they knew how difficult Helen was finding life while the breadwinner was away. Their friendship was to last more than forty years.

Eventually Helen was forced to sell the house and business in order to pay creditors. She moved to a smaller house and to make ends meet did all sorts of work. She took in washing and shirt-repairing, reversing collars and cuffs; she patched sheets and for all these jobs she charged one penny per repair. This and eight shillings a week army pension was the family's only income. Life was indeed a struggle, but Helen always said that God and Spirit were with her at all times. When she was at her lowest ebb, some friend would turn up with help. It seemed to her that through these wonderful friends God was saying, "I do love you. I do care about you." She made a promise to use her gifts, whatever they may be, to help people at all times. It was a promise she kept, serving with her natural gifts until her death.

Not long after Helen had moved to the new house, she had a visitor. She answered a knock on her door one morning to find a kind, fresh- faced woman, holding a bunch of flowers.

"I thought I'd welcome you to your new home," said the visitor. "My name is MacLain." The words all came out in a rush.

Helen smiled at "Auntie Mac", as she was to become affectionately known to the family. "Why look so embarrassed?" she asked. "Do come in. It's nice of you to call."

Over a cup of tea Mac admitted to her new friend that she had heard about her being a medium. While she was talking, Helen had seen clairvoyantly a little boy about three years old, standing by Mac's chair. When she stopped talking, Helen asked if she knew a child of that age in Spirit.

Mac nodded. "Yes," she said.

"His name is David and he is your son," Helen went on.

"That's true. He died a year ago with diphtheria."

"He says you haven't to worry about Elaine. It's only a cold and she'll be all right. He says he's glad you've met Mama Duncan."

Later, when this child materialised, he always referred to Helen as Mama Duncan.

Mac told Helen how she had been widowed and lost her little son, all within a year. "But I sometimes see them when I'm in the garden," she added happily. "Well, I must go. I've left Elaine, my daughter, in bed. But you say it's only a cold."

"Do come again when you can," said Helen and Mac hurried down the street humming to herself. Meeting Mrs Duncan and having it all confirmed that her husband and son were watching over her and Elaine had made her feel happy and elated. Suddenly out loud she said, "Isn't God wonderful!"

Chapter 9

Trials and Tribulations

When at last Henry came home, very much thinner and still not a fit man; Helen took a job in the bleach mills. The hours suited the family's needs, but Helen found it tough. Starting at 5 a.m. and working until 8 a.m. she would then rush home, wake the children, feed and wash them and send them off to school. Then she would attend to the baby before rushing back to work until 2 p.m., at which time she would return home, do her housework and look after Henry before getting tea for the girls.

The work was cold and back-breaking. Often Helen's overalls were frozen to her body. Working in those conditions eventually took its toll. One Sunday she had got up early to light the boiler in the outhouse. Sunday was her only day off, so she always did the family washing. She did not feel too good and had a nagging pain in her back. She kept going because she knew she had to, but gradually she began to feel worse. As she tried to take the washing from the boiler she collapsed on the stone floor with an excruciating pain. She lay waiting for the pain to subside and praying for help. Unable to get up, she managed to crawl back to the door of the house, where the children found her when they came home from Sunday School.

It was yet another dash to hospital for the Duncan family.

Helen was found to be suffering from kidney paralysis. The treatment in those days was to wrap the patient's body in very hot blankets in the hope that heat would start the kidneys functioning again. This was hard work for the nurses and primitive compared with modern methods, the patient's recovery being mostly in the hands of God. Helen's God smiled upon her and she recovered, but the effect of her illness was with her for the rest of her life.

That life was full of trials and tribulations for Helen, but she never complained. They had food and a roof over their heads. What more was needed? It must be said that she was a good housewife, able to make meals from very little. She knew a market gardener from whom she could buy "two pennorth" of vegetables, which consisted of swedes, carrots, leeks, cabbage and potatoes, enough to last a week. At the grocer's she would by "one pennorth" of peas and barley and any bacon ends and bones he might have. From this she would make one of the children's favourite meals. Christened 'Mealy Pudding' by them, it consisted of oatmeal cooked with the bacon ends, served with mashed swede and potatoes. Broth was another family filler. The children would leave all the peas until the end to see who had the most in their dish. Many arguments ensued if one child thought the other had too many peas in the dish.

Once again Helen became pregnant. To everyone's joy the baby was a boy, named Henry after his father. The girls were delighted with their baby brother, wanting to take turns to mother him. He was a lovely boy, all ten pounds of him. As he grew older the girls would laugh triumphantly as he learned each new word or took his first faltering steps. At about this time it became obvious that one of Helen's psychic gifts was the power to heal sickness in others. It was an ability which at times had troublesome consequences.

When Isabella was once in great pain from a large

swelling which had developed on her face, Helen, with a mother's love, tried to comfort her. As the child continued to cry, Helen pleaded that the pain should be eased. "Please take this from her and give it to me," she prayed. "I am stronger and able to bear it."

Even as the family watched, Helen's face slowly started to swell and redden, while Isabella's swelling started to recede. It was the first time the children had witnessed any kind of psychic phenomena and it was not to be the last by any means. The outcome of that particular episode was that the next day Helen had to visit the dentist for a tooth extraction while Isabella was back to her normal self!

Always with her healing gift, Helen was to find that whenever she came into contact with sickness, she took upon herself the symptoms of the patient. Another instance of this, but with not such a happy outcome, was a result of Helen's first visit to a Spiritualist Church. She knew nothing of Spiritualism, having accepted her psychic gifts as natural, with a little understanding that her body make-up must be different from others because of the psychic force which surrounded it.

Helen and Henry arrived at the meeting and took their places. When Helen asked Henry what was going on, he explained that the evening was to be a demonstration of clairvoyance. As he was telling her about procedure the medium came in through a door at the back of the rostrum. Helen immediately became upset. As the meeting progressed she became increasingly agitated. Henry knew things were far from right and he took her hand to comfort her. She gripped his hand so tightly that he had to stop himself from calling out to her to let go. When he asked her what was wrong she answered, "Can't you see it then? Oh, God help him!"

She became so distressed that Henry stood up and made

an apology to the medium before ushering out his now nearly hysterical wife from the meeting. All the way home Helen cried and wrung her hands together, saying over and over again, "Help him. Oh, please God, help him!"

At last they reached home and Henry gave his wife some tea. After what seemed like ages he calmed her a little and although still upset and crying she told him what she had seen.

"When that man came on to the rostrum there was a figure like a large monkey following him," she said. "As he walked about, this thing followed him. The monkey thing had what looked like a noose and he was trying to put it over the man's head."

Helen again burst into an uncontrollable fit of tears. Through her sobs Henry could hear her saying, "It will kill him. Oh God, it will kill him."

Henry looked into her anguished eyes and felt helpless.

"Henry, we must help him. Promise. Please promise."

He promised to try.

Next day he made enquiries and discovered that the medium was a local man. He gave the address to Helen, who set out to find it as soon as she could. As she drew near the house she saw two women standing by the gate. They stopped talking as she reached them and one of them asked if she could help Helen.

"I would just like to speak to Mr Black*," said Helen.

"I'm sorry, but he's not at home just now," said the woman. "Can I give him a message?"

"Well, I really must talk to him," replied Helen. "It's so important."

"Yes, it's always important," said Mrs Black.

"I don't think you understand," said Helen, who did not

* (The name is fictitious to avoid embarrassment to living relatives).

like her hostile attitude.

"Oh, yes I do, my dear. Have you lost a loved one, maybe you're having marital problems?"

"I certainly have not," retorted Helen. "I have come here to try and help your husband."

"You?" laughed Mrs Black.

"Yes," whispered Helen, suddenly feeling unsure of herself. "Please remember that at all costs I came here to help if I could."

She then felt obliged to tell what she had seen at the church. Had she not received her psychic gifts in order to help others? In a much firmer voice she told Mrs Black her name and address and exactly what she had seen at the meeting. "Please tell your husband before it is too late," she added.

Mrs Black looked at Helen and laughed.

"You're mad, woman!" she said. "You should be locked away!"

She turned and walked towards the house.

"Please listen," Helen called after her. "If you need me, remember my address."

Without turning round, Mrs Black entered her house and banged the door.

Helen returned home with a heavy heart, saying to herself, "She will need me sooner than she realises."

Family matters and another pregnancy took this matter from her mind. The baby, a second boy, was born prematurely and weighed only 3½ pounds. In those days, before modern infant care and incubators, the best care was love and prayers. Peter spent the first few weeks of his life in a cardboard box which was lined with cotton wool. Henry and Helen took it in turns to feed their new son with an eyedropper, as he was too weak to suckle. Love, constant devotion and prayer, saw the little mite grow stronger and thrive. Indeed, in later years Peter became a teaching signalman in the Royal Navy and served his country during the 1939-45 war. But that is leaping forward.

Peter was three months old when his mother answered her doorbell one day to find a distraught woman asking for help. Memories of eleven months before came back and Helen recognised the woman as Mrs Black. She kindly asked her in, but before she was even seated Mrs Black burst out, "It's my husband. The doctors have committed him to the asylum. You see, he kept saying someone was trying to kill him."

Helen told her to be calm and tell her the whole story.

"He had very bad headaches," said Mrs Black. "In the end the doctors were afraid he would try to kill himself, so they put him in the asylum for his own safety."

Helen did her best to comfort the woman and when she promised to visit her husband in the asylum next day, Mrs Black thanked her and left.

When Helen saw Mr Black in the asylum the following day, she was shocked to see the deterioration in his condition from the time she had last seen him. At the meeting he had been a sturdy 5 feet 8 inches, at least 12 stone in weight. Before her now was a man who was drawn, haggard and just skin and bone, obviously in great pain. Placing her hands on his head, Helen silently prayed that he be given peace of mind. She sat with him for some time until she felt that he had fallen into a deep sleep. As she left the hospital she developed a dreadful headache and by the time she reached home the pain was so intense she could hardly see.

Seeing his wife so white and drawn, Henry made her go straight to bed with some tablets and a hot drink. She appeared to go to sleep after a short while, so he left her in order to attend to the children's tea. After about an hour he heard her cry out, "Oh no! Please God, no!"

Rushing to the bedroom he saw Helen holding her head in her hands, rocking backwards and forwards in great pain.

"What's wrong, lass?" he asked.

In an anguished voice Helen replied, "Help me, help me, Hen. Something is pressing on my head like a vice."

Henry immediately realised that Helen had taken on herself the condition of the poor man she had visited in the asylum, also that there was a possibility that an evil entity was trying to take possession of her. He took the family Bible from its place in a drawer and sitting beside Helen he opened the book at random. He read loudly Chapter 4, verses 1-6 from Corinthians II, the page at which the Bible had opened.

Years later, as he related this incident, the drama of it still seemed to fill him with awe. As he finished reading, Helen's nose started to bleed, blood spurting rather like a pump. The room went ice cold. He felt he was no longer alone with Helen, but that also into their bedroom had come something evil. Sweating with fear and still holding the Bible, he recited the 23rd Psalm. In the stillness which followed the words of the Psalm there was a loud bang, then absolute silence.

The bleeding from Helen's nose stopped and she sat up. Henry brought a bowl of water and towels and helped his wife to wash and change her clothes. After being made comfortable she fell into a natural sleep.

Some weeks later, Helen and Henry were told of Mr Black's passing. He had had his tea and free of pain, had shortly afterwards gone to sleep. Some time later a nurse noticed that he had stopped breathing. On checking, it was found that he was dead.

The timing of this incident and the estimated time of his death exactly coincided with the stopping of Helen's nose bleed.

Chapter 10

Helping and Serving

Through all the years and all the troubles, the Thursday circle, which was resumed as soon as Henry recovered from his heart attack, continued to sit. It now consisted of Henry and the Murray brothers Jim and Frank, Mrs MacLain and Joe Sauter.

Mrs Mac' was a good psychic. She often told the story of how one morning while busy doing her housework she heard her little dead son call, "Mummy, Mama Duncan needs some flowers."

In her mind she answered him: "All right son, I'll take them when I finish the cleaning."

"No, Mummy. Please - she needs them now," came the boy's voice again.

His plea was so urgent that she said, "Very well. I'll go now." She went into her garden and picked some flowers before walking down the street to the Duncan house.

Helen had been busy cleaning and polishing. "A pretty vase of flowers on the table would look nice," she had remarked to her sister-in-law and long-time friend, Jean.

"Why don't you ask your spooky friends to bring you some?" laughed Jean.

Smiling softly Helen said, "I'll do just that."

Ten minutes later, Mac arrived with a bunch of flowers. Jean's eyes and mouth opened wide as Mac explained how she had been compelled to bring them.

The circle was progressing well. Due to the sincerity and psychic ability of the sitters materialisation was slowly being achieved. A hand would sometimes appear on the small table in the corner and a head which was recognised by one of the sitters as his father, appeared more than once.

As in all small communities, word soon spread and it was not long before the stories of Helen's psychic gifts began to circulate. Many came for help and advice and none was ever refused. Although some looked upon it as fortune-telling, there were many whose first knowledge of the survival of spirit after death and beyond, came from the lips of Helen Duncan. Evidence that loved ones who had passed into Spirit could still love and care for those on earth influenced many to a way of life which has its own reward.

One day Henry arrived home from work accompanied by a gentleman who was a stranger to Helen. All he said to her was, "He's very much in need of help. Can you help him, lass?"

"I can but try," Helen replied.

She asked the man into the parlour, where she usually saw the people who needed help. In a house full of children this was the one room kept tidy and set aside for such visitors. The man was very impressed by Helen's evidence of survival. He told both Henry and Helen after the sitting that no one outside his family could possibly have known some of the things passed on through Helen's mediumship. Before she ended her message to this stranger, Helen said, "You came here because you are in a great difficulty over a business matter. I don't know what it means, but the gentleman I can see standing beside you says you will understand. He is showing me an egg with two yolks and the figure three.

This gentleman is very close to you."

After the man had left, Helen asked Henry who he was.

"I don't know," he replied, going on to explain that at lunchtime he had gone to the pub for a quick snack and had noticed the man sitting alone, looking very worried. Henry had felt compelled to go and talk to him.

Initially, the stranger was reluctant to enter into conversation, but gradually the sincerity of Henry's wish to help must have made an impression. The man explained that his business, a gentleman's outfitters, was in financial difficulties.

"Maybe my wife can help you," offered Henry. "She's a good clairvoyant."

"Oh, I don't think so," the man demurred.

"Och, away man, you have nothing to lose and maybe much to gain, so why don't you try?"

That is how Henry came to bring him home. As they were both used to this sort of encounter with complete strangers, neither of the Duncans thought any more about the episode.

A week later they were just settling down for the evening when there was an unexpected knock at the door. When Helen opened it, there was the stranger from the previous week, holding a brown paper parcel. He asked if he might come in and talk to her and her husband. Of course, Helen invited him in and at first, as the three looked at each other, there was an embarrassing silence, which Henry broke by asking the man to sit down. Helen, in her usual way of putting people at their ease, made them all a cup of tea.

As they relaxed the man explained that he had come to express his thanks for the help he had received the previous week. Both Helen and Henry looked at him, not understanding what he meant. Turning to Helen he said, "Let me explain. The day I met your husband I had a letter from my accountant saying that the business was in such a bad state I could be facing bankruptcy, which was why I was so worried.

"You told me about an egg with two yolks and the figure three. It came from a gentleman in Spirit who was very close to me. Well, my partner liked a flutter on the horses in big races and when I got home, everything you had told me seemed so accurate that I checked the runners in the Grand National, due to be run on the Saturday.

"A horse called Double Life was running and as this was the only name which fitted with the 'double yolks' you gave me, I put everything I had on it and it came up! I'm happy, my accountant is happy and now all that remains is for me to share my happiness with you both."

As he said this he rose to his feet and handed Henry the parcel which he had been holding ever since he came in. Then he took a small box from his pocket and handed it to Helen.

"God bless you and yours for the help you have given me," he said. As he took his leave, Helen and Henry were speechless. As they went to the door Henry suddenly realised he did not even know the man's name. He pointed this out to the stranger, who replied. "What does that matter? We met, you saw I needed help and you gave me your hand in friendship for which I will always be grateful. Good-night, my friend."

He closed the door behind him and they never saw nor heard of him again.

When Helen opened the small box she found it contained a gold watch, inscribed on the back "Helen Duncan. Double Life", with the date. In 1956 the watch was given to Helen's granddaughter, but was very quickly lost. The family believed it was meant only for Helen and it was not intended that anyone else should own it.

Henry's gift was a 'Swallow' raincoat, which at that time was one of the most expensive makes of gentleman's raincoats.

Upon reflection, the stranger must have felt that Helen's message and survival evidence was exceptional for him to have risked all he had on one race.

Many were helped, many were grateful, but when the need was reversed, many forgot.

Chapter 11

The Struggles for Perfection

Week in, week out, the five sitters gathered every Thursday at the Duncan home. Things seemed to be progressing well and at times full figures had materialised. Although the shapes were rather grotesque, the evidence given by Spirit with those badly developed forms was good and could be accepted by the sitter concerned. Spirit control explained that as progress was made in the development of their instrument, Helen Duncan, the required correction to the phenomena would be made possible and recognisable spirit forms would materialise.

Before the progress was made there were many disturbing incidents. One was so frightening that all the sitters ran from the house, leaving Henry and the entranced Helen alone.

It had been a beautiful July day in 1926. Helen and Henry's seventh child, Gena, born two days before their wedding anniversary, was a contented six weeks old. It was always Helen's practice to keep the youngest close to her, even during the circle. Each of the babies in turn had always slept peacefully during the time the circle was in progress.

This particular day, Helen felt uneasy and as evening approached, she mentioned it to Henry. She told him she would put Gena upstairs with the other children.

"What for?" asked Henry. "She'll be all right."

"I don't know. I don't feel happy somehow," Helen replied.

She had her way and after the children had been given tea, washed and put to bed, she and Henry sat quietly for the hour before the circle was due to start. This relaxation is important for a physical medium. During the time the body relaxes, Spirit can build up the power it needs.

At the usual time the sitters took their places, forming a half-circle around Helen, who sat by the fireplace. As it was such a warm evening the fire was not alight. Helen soon went into trance. Suddenly, the sewing machine, which was always kept in the corner of the room furthest from the fireplace and fully locked because of the children, began to vibrate. The lid was thrown open with a loud bang and the machine then moved around the room, coming behind the sitters and pushing against them.

By this time all present felt that something evil had come into their midst. Suddenly the whole fireplace was pulled out, crashing into the room.

"Oh, God help us!" shouted Joe and as one all the sitters fled from the house. Henry scrambled over the pile of rubble to reach Helen, who was covered in dust and soot and in deep distress, bleeding from the nose, ears and mouth.

Henry switched on the light and could hardly believe his wife was still alive when he saw the extent of the damage. The fire surround could only have missed her by inches. Tiles, wood and bricks lay broken and scattered on the floor. He thanked God that just a moment before the circle had started, Helen had complained of a draught from the chimney and had moved her chair a little back from its usual place.

Helen moaned and as he touched her she said, "What

happened? Oh dear, look at the mess!" She promptly burst into tears. Henry's first concern was for her.

"All that matters is that you're all right, lass," he said.

Looking at her husband Helen said, "Thank God I put the wee one upstairs." Each knew what the other was thinking. Henry helped Helen from her chair and out of the room.

"You go and clean yourself up and I'll see to this mess. All right, lass?"

As he started to clear up he heard a timid knock on the front door.

"I'll get it, Nell, you carry on," he called. At the door stood Frank and Jim Murray. "Come in, you two," said Henry.

"Are you all right?" said Frank sheepishly.

"Yes, but Nell's not so good. Come and see," answered Henry. "Come and see the mess."

When they saw the state of the room the brothers gasped. "What on earth did that?" asked Jim, more to himself than to the others. It took the three men most of the night to clear up.

Helen meanwhile had washed and changed and prepared tea and sandwiches for them all. As they sat at the kitchen table they discussed the events of the evening. Poor Helen could only listen, as she had no first hand knowledge of what took place at any of the séances. She was always in trance and depending upon her husband and the spirit helpers to protect her.

"We must have failed somewhere," she said.

"I think I know," said Henry. "In fact, I'm sure I do." Looking at Jim and Frank he continued, "Do you remember Dr Williams telling us that at all times we must test Spirit?

Well, if they came in love they would not have done this and if they were evil they would not have come if we had read a verse from the Bible, said a prayer or sung a hymn, for we would have protected ourselves with love and the power of God."

The friends then agreed that all future sittings would be started in this way. The following Thursday the sitters arrived early. About fifteen minutes before the circle was due to start, Henry spoke to them all.

"You know friends, why we have gathered a little earlier, so there is no need for us to go over last week's séance, but I will take this opportunity to thank you all for coming back after such a frightening experience. From now on I will open our circle with a prayer, followed by the Lord's Prayer said by all of us. Then we will sing the 23rd Psalm. Do you all agree?"

"Yes," they answered together.

The séance began as Henry had directed. During the last verse of the Psalm, the voice of Dr Williams joined the sitters' voices and when the singing ended he said, "Good evening."

"Good evening, Dr Williams," they replied.

"Duncan, can you hear me?" he asked.

"Yes," Henry replied.

"I must apologise for last week because I feel I failed you. This sick force came in. Can you and your good lady forgive me?"

"Yes, of course," they answered.

"We too failed her because we had not done as you told us," said Henry. "Are we correct now?" I

"Yes and thank you," said Dr Williams. "It is now time to move on further with our work. I would like to have a cabinet for Mrs Duncan to sit in. This will contain the power we build. With this power we can make the ectoplasm which is required to produce the phenomena of materialisation. Do you understand?"

"Yes," Henry said. "But what kind of cabinet do you want us to make? A wooden structure?"

"No, no. You don't have to do that. Just fasten a black curtain across a corner of the room. Place an upright chair inside the curtain and we will do the rest," explained Dr Williams.

He went on to instruct the sitters to try to obtain a red light or lamp and a trumpet. The latter would be used to help the voices of loved ones who had passed into spirit to talk to those still on earth.

During the weeks that followed, the friends set about carrying out Dr Williams' instructions. The trumpet was easy to come by; they made a thin piece of aluminium into a cone shape. To make it visible in the dark, two bands each one inch wide were painted on it. One band was an inch from the mouthpiece and the other an inch from the bottom. This original trumpet is still in use in a circle in Wiltshire, having been given to a Mr Averill by Helen some years before her passing.

The red light proved to be a more difficult problem. Many trials and errors were made, including an old railway lamp lit by paraffin, the fumes from which nearly overcame all the sitters. At last Henry found a suitable light. He made a small square box, fitted with an ordinary light fitting, the top of the box consisting of a piece of red glass which slotted in so that removal was possible. Dimming, if required, could be achieved by placing a handkerchief over the glass top.

Development was now being accomplished at a very

high rate. Even the task of caring for their home and children and earning a living was not allowed to interfere with Helen and Henry's weekly appointment with their spirit friends and helpers. Voices were now coming through each week. Indeed, sometimes two or three voices could be heard talking at the same time. The trumpet would circle the room at great speed, so that the sitters would often have difficulty following it with their eyes. As the voices increased, Henry introduced a second trumpet. The two trumpets would move round the room in different directions. Sometimes one would be high up near the ceiling while the other would be close to the sitters as a particular loved one spoke to one of them. At other times both trumpets would be near different sitters and two separate spirit voices could be heard, giving advice or comfort. The two trumpets made fraud or trickery an absolute impossibility.

One evening the voice of Dr Williams addressed the sitters and asked if they felt ready to learn what could be done with ectoplasm. All answered in the affirmative. They were instructed to watch the cabinet carefully.

As he spoke, out through the curtain enclosing the corner of the room which served as Helen's cabinet came a substance not unlike cheesecloth or butter muslin. The material continued to flow until there seemed to the sitters to be at least ten yards in a soft pile in the room. Henry asked if he could touch it and was told he could. He said afterwards that it was dry and soft to touch. The other sitters remarked that there was no odour. Through the opening of the curtains they could see Helen sitting in her hard-backed chair and the ectoplasm flowing from her nose and ears. They were amazed to see the substance flowing down the front of her dress on to her lap, then down on to the floor and out to the centre of the room. The curtains were drawn together and the substance started to recede until the entire volume had gone back into the cabinet.

There now appeared a rod about three feet long. It came all round the sitters and stopped at Jim Murray. Dr Williams told him to take hold of the rod and bang it on the floor. When he had done this, he was asked if the rod felt solid.

"Solid as steel," he replied.

He was then told to place the rod so that it rested on two chairs two feet apart and to sit in the centre of the rod. He did as directed and was lifted up above the heads of the other sitters, who were asked to stand up and check that there was no rope or anything else holding Jim up.

The sitters were very careful in their examination of any spirit phenomena. Joe Sauter and Frank Murray stood on chairs to make sure nothing was holding Jim from above. The voice asked if they were certain there was nothing holding Jim up so high, "no material substance", as Dr Williams called it. He then thanked them and told Jim he would be lowered and would they please watch carefully.

Jim was lowered gently to the floor, the rod disappeared and Jim was left standing in the middle of the circle. Dr Williams' voice then said, "I will leave you for the present. Good-night and God bless you all."

During this stage of development much phenomena was witnessed - voices, lights and the continuing development of the ectoplasm, which at times resembled a spider's web and at other times solid steel.

Dr Williams explained that the crude forms which were sometimes moulded from the ectoplasm were not intended to resemble deceased persons at this early stage. The purpose was to perfect the process. Any advance and progress would be made possible through the continued development of the mediumship. Eventually the materialised forms began to take on a proper physical appearance and began to appear less artificial or unreal.

Eighteen months after Henry's return from hospital and the resumption of the circle, there came a new development. After the opening prayer, Dr Williams introduced a gentleman by the name of Donald. The sitters were informed that Donald would take over the duties of control, or guide as some people call them. This spirit control was a formidable character of whom Henry did not approve. He completely took over the running of the circle and by sheer force of personality seemed to dominate all. If Henry complained about procedure, Donald would inform him that he knew what he was doing. It was the annoying things which Donald asked the medium to do which upset Henry. He would begin the séance by opening the curtains of the cabinet, standing at one side while the entranced Helen sat in her upright chair. He would then ask the sitters if they could see them both, after which Helen would be asked to stand up, sit down, walk around the room, then return to sit again on her chair in the cabinet while Donald remained beside her chair. In between all this activity however, he could and did give absolute proof of survival.

Around this time the sitters were instructed to invite different people to join the circle as visitors. It was explained that it was important if evidence given by Spirit was to be proved, it had to be given to as wide a public as possible. Each week two or three visitors were invited to join the regular sitters for this purpose. By this time materialisation was a regular occurrence.

As each materialised spirit appeared, Donald could give full name, cause of so-called death and date of passing. At one sitting two young ladies invited by Mrs Mac were the reason for Donald being recalled from his position as control.

Helen was once again pregnant and had suffered kidney pain. She had been prescribed by her doctor a medicine containing morphine. The bottle of medicine was kept on a high shelf in the parlour, out of reach of the children.

At this particular séance, Donald left the cabinet and approached the two girls, then proceeding to give them remarkable evidence. He told them the names and addresses of both their parents and where they worked. One of the young ladies was very beautiful and Donald became very personal about this, which made Henry very angry. He told Donald to behave himself or he would stop the séance. Donald replied, "You can't do anything to me, for I am not dependent on her." He pointed to Helen, sitting in the cabinet in deep trance.

Turning away from the sitters he continued, "Watch. I'll show you." He quickly moved to the shelf where the medicine stood and taking the bottle in his hand was about to open it when a voice was heard from the cabinet, "Donald. You must return immediately. You have gone far enough."

Donald replaced the bottle and returned to the cabinet. The sitters then heard what appeared to be a heated argument between two distinct male voices, but afterwards no one could remember any words. Suddenly the curtains parted and there stood a handsome bearded man, well over six feet tall, looking even taller beside the seated Helen. Stepping forward, this spirit introduced himself in a clear voice as Albert Stewart. He explained he had been born in Scotland, but had emigrated to Australia with his parents, where he had been a trade apprentice as a pattern-maker. He had passed to spirit in 1913 at the age of thirty-three. He turned to Henry and said, "Mr Duncan, we have sent Donald back as he was not doing his job properly, but I assure you that from now on you will have nothing to fear.

Together we will move forward to a better understanding and better phenomena. Before we close the séance, will you please tell Mrs Duncan (Albert always referred to Helen as Mrs Duncan) to have Gena moved from the doorway of the hospital ward. We are concerned for her lungs. I will say au revoir until we meet again."

Chapter 12

Two Kinds of Test

That evening after the sitters had left, Henry told Helen of the events at the séance. Helen was disturbed when told what Albert Stewart had said regarding Gena.

Gena had been born with a lymph oedema of the right hand and arm. It had been a difficult delivery, as Helen had gone into an eclamptic fit when the baby was partially born. In her concern for the baby's safety and knowing of the other child, Etta, suffering from dislocated limbs during birth, the midwife placed her fingers under the baby's arms to complete delivery, but had put more pressure than she intended on the arms. As soon as she realised the baby had been injured by pressure, the midwife had her taken to hospital a few hours after birth. Gena was kept in hospital for two weeks and then the parents were told that nothing could be done until she was older, possibly at one year.

Now Gena was one year old and had been in hospital two months. Her arm was elevated and excess fluid drained away. So far there had not been much success with this treatment and as soon as the splint was removed the limb had again swollen and filled with fluid. Then Gena contracted measles, so was retained in hospital.

The morning after the séance when Albert Stewart first appeared, Helen visited the hospital to find Gena's cot just inside the doorway of the ward. She noticed the baby looked far from well. She was hot and flushed and crying. Helen called the nurse on duty and asked what was wrong with her baby. The nurse replied that she was running a temperature, but was otherwise all right.

"My baby is not all right and I would like to see the doctor now, please," said Helen sternly.

The nurse turned away saying, "Oh, you mothers!"

Again Helen demanded to see a doctor. As she waited she noticed that Gena had difficulty in breathing. She took her hand in hers and felt how hot it was. As the nurse returned, Helen asked where the doctor was.

"He will be coming soon," was the reply.

By now Helen was both worried and angry at the delay.

"You had better get him now. My bairn has pneumonia and I want her moved from this draughty doorway."

"I'm sure you're wrong," replied the nurse, "You aren't a doctor, you know."

"I know you had better move now, or by all I hold dear, I'll report this to the Head of the hospital," retorted Helen, who was now very angry. She was aware that someone had failed to report a rise in the baby's temperature and that a doctor should have been called earlier because this was a known complication of measles. Finally a doctor arrived to see the baby and the requested move was made. In fact Gena was very ill with pneumonia, but recovered. She was the only one of Helen's surviving six children to follow her mother into the Spiritualist movement.

Helen's pregnancy this time resulted in the birth of another boy, but Baby Alex only survived thirteen months.

Helen had asked a young girl to look after the children while she went to do the family shopping. Alex, who was teething and had a cold, was crying and fretful, she decided to dress him and take him to meet his mother, thinking the outing would stop him crying. She dressed him a wool suit which she found in a basket of clean linen. It was a cold blustery day and they had gone quite a way before meeting Helen on her return. When she met them and noticed the baby's suit she asked Mary where she found it.

"In the clothes basket in the kitchen," came the reply.

"Oh, my God!" said Helen. "Those clothes were not properly dry."

"Honestly, Mrs Duncan, they felt dry to me," said Mary.

Hurrying as fast as possible, Helen said the clothes in the basket had only been washed the previous evening and hung on the pulley line for the night, so could not possibly by dry. As soon as she got home Helen stripped little Alex and gave him a hot bath, but fate was again cruel to Helen and another of her babies was taken from her. Baby Alex developed double pneumonia and within a week he was laid to rest beside his sister Etta.

The children were all upset by the loss of Alex. Nan, the second daughter, who was only ten but very mature for her age, would take the other children out, away from their grieving parents. They would all go to the park to play and Nan would explain that Mummy and Daddy had sore hearts because Alex had gone to heaven and they missed him very much.

"Will they get better?" asked Lilian.

"Oh yes. With our loving they will get better," replied the sage little Nan.

By this time Helen had become well known as a clairvoyant, trance and materialisation medium and now found herself starting her ninth pregnancy. The shock of Alex's death, together with the pressure of all the work she was undertaking, made her very ill and weak. The family doctor stated she was in no fit state to bear another child and told Henry she must have an abortion and at the same time be sterilised.

Henry had great difficulty persuading Helen that the doctor was right. It was only when he told her that the doctor had also said she would not survive another birth and then their other children would be motherless that Helen agreed to go into the hospital. She was admitted as soon as she agreed and the operation was carried out. Later Henry was to tell his daughter Gena that it was a very anxious time for him, as Helen was extremely ill. When she recovered her strength it was decided that the family should move to Thornton Heath, near London. As Helen's development had continued it was agreed that she should be tested as a medium by the London Psychic Centre.

On one of her many visits to the Psychic Centre, as she and Henry walked up the stairs, Henry remarked upon a man walking in front of them.

"I wonder who he is?" he whispered.

Helen looked at the man's back before answering.

"I don't know, but I don't like the vibrations around him." She stopped walking and put her arm out to touch Henry. "Oh God, Henry," she added. "Watch that one doesn't knife you in the back."

As Henry looked at Helen he noticed her face had drained of colour. In fact, she looked quite ill. "What do you mean lass?" he asked.

"I have no idea, but I do know he'll try to hurt you," she answered, close to tears.

Later, when they learned the man's identity, Helen's words often came into Henry's mind. He had much reason to remember the name of Mr Harry Price.

Whatever her initial feelings, during the period of 1930

to 1931, Helen was to give four materialisation séances for Harry Price, who had a tenancy on the fourth floor of the Spiritualist Alliance Headquarters at 16 Queensberry Place, in Kensington. He had a different approach from that of the Psychic Union regarding the evidence of spiritual phenomena and for this reason, both he and his methods were at variance with those of the Union.

Helen had gone to London to be tested by the Union, but both she and Henry, although reluctant, felt they could not refuse Price's request for sittings. After the first séance Price told Helen he was very pleased by the evidence which had been given, but felt he would like to make some more tests. The Duncans agreed and at one such test séance he cut a piece of ectoplasm (with permission of the spirit control), for chemical analysis. He took details of the analysis[1] to Hannen Swaffer, who was already a well known Fleet Street journalist. In his office at the 'Daily Express', "Swaff", as he was known to his friends in the Spiritualist movement, dictated to his secretary a column on the composition of ectoplasm. Price supplied the technical details from the analysis he had completed. The article was never published by the 'Daily Express'. At that time it was extremely difficult to persuade any newspaper to print anything which might appear to favour Spiritualism.

Price made repeated requests for a special test sitting with Helen and she finally agreed. "If only to be rid of the man," she told Henry.

When requesting this special sitting, Price always finished his request with, "I will not harm you - I only want to make a special test under my own supervision."

On the day appointed for this special test Helen could not throw off the feeling that something was wrong. On arrival she and Henry were shown into a room which had been prepared for the test. The chairs on which the sitters were to be, had wires round each leg, attached to what appeared to be an electrical appliance. Price explained that the wires would be attached to the sitters and also to Mrs Duncan. If anyone left a chair, an alarm would ring. Helen was nervous.

"I don't like it, Hen," she said. "I'm frightened."

"It will be all right, lass," he assured her.

As Helen took her seat, Price went up close to her and whispered, "We would like you to disrobe."

This was the last straw for Helen. Her initial fear and mistrust of this man, the frightening array of electrical gadgets and now to be told she would have to undress, was too much. She turned and ran from the room, down the four flights of stairs and only stopped when she reached the street.

It was here she was found by Henry and the two men who accompanied him. She was crying and clutching the railings for support. It took a great deal of persuasion before she would go back into the building and eventually back into the test room. As they entered Henry heard Price talking about fraud. Price turned to him and asked him to turn out his pockets.

"I certainly will not. Whatever for?" asked Henry.

By this time Helen had found both her voice and her temper.

"How dare you!" she screamed at Price. She lashed out to strike him but accidentally hit Henry, who had moved closer to calm her. Henry reeled backwards and fell. Helen grabbed him and they both left the room as quickly as possible.

"Well, that's the last we'll see of Mr Harry Price," said Henry as they reached the street.

"Don't be too sure of that," replied the still upset Helen.

"I told you to watch him. He's not interested in Spiritualism, but only tried to prove that everyone is cheating and using trickery."

Shortly after that encounter with Price, the Duncans were told of his claims that Helen was a fraud. Price persisted in his statements that the ectoplasm or phenomena was achieved by regurgitation.

Price's theory of regurgitation[2] becomes laughable when it is noted that he himself reported that on one occasion, under test conditions and after Helen had been subjected to a thorough gynaecological examination, he admitted that examination had failed to disclose anything. The phenomena occurred in spite of everything she had been put through. Yet Price persisted in his theory and, to help to make it all the more plausible, he cited medieval and modern cases where it was said that people had regurgitated live frogs and solid objects. However, never did Price cite one instance where anyone had regurgitated anything even remotely resembling cheesecloth.

1 *"The Case of Helen Duncan" by Maurice Barbanell*
2 *"The Case of Helen Duncan" by Maurice Barbanell.*

Chapter 13

The Working Medium

When Helen finally satisfied the Psychic Union's varied and extensive tests, she was granted her diploma. This meant that she could now serve the Union as a qualified medium at its many churches throughout the country. Both Henry and Helen felt that for the family's sake they should return to Edinburgh and from there decide on how best to plan the future.

They found a top floor flat in Broughton Place, Edinburgh, a tenement building, which was the only type of accommodation available to rent at that time. Working for the Union would mean a considerable amount of travelling and being away from home and Helen felt reluctant to travel alone. She always felt more confident when not separated from Henry. For this reason they both thought that the children would be better cared for at a boarding school. They found a suitable council run school at Kelso, where the children settled in quite happily. Bella, the oldest girl, had left school at fourteen and was working, but Henry and Helen felt she was still too young to be left alone, so they decided to employ Mary, a young girl they both knew, to look after the home and be company for Bella. The arrangement seemed to work quite well.

The first Easter, Helen and Henry, returning from

Bristol from yet another working journey, visited the children at school before returning to the flat. They arrived with presents, Easter Eggs, sweets and fruit, not only for their own children, but for the other children too. They all had a lovely afternoon, picnicking and playing in the beautiful school grounds. Tired but happy, they went back to the flat to have tea with Bella and Mary.

They had arranged with their old friends, Jim and Frank Murray, Dr Allan, an African friend and one or two others, to hold a séance on that visit home. As soon as all had settled down, Albert came through and in his inimitable way, wished them all 'Good Evening'. Then he immediately said he would not be staying, but had only come to speak to his friend, Dr Allan.*

"My friend," called Albert. "Will you please come to me?"

As the doctor reached the cabinet, Albert opened the black curtain stretched across the corner of the room and said, "I hope you are not afraid of me?"

"Of you, Albert? No, never. You are more alive than some I know," replied the doctor and both men laughed.

"No more jest," whispered Albert. "I am worried about Jim Murray. I fear he has an ulcer on his face. Will you examine him for me? I will come and talk to him alone before he returns to Dundee. Now, if you will allow me, I will say Good-night to my friends."

The doctor then left the cabinet and returned to his seat as Albert called his usual "Au revoir" to the other sitters.

When the séance ended and the friends had their normal kindly hospitality from the Duncans, it was an easy matter

---

* *I was once present at a séance where Albert described Dr Allan, who was a full blooded African negro, as a man with the brightest, whitest heart he had ever met. (Gena Brealey.)*

for the doctor to stay behind when the other sitters left.

Frank and Jim Murray were staying in the flat that night, having travelled from Dundee especially for the séance. The doctor told Jim that Albert had asked him to have a close look at the sore on his face. Jim had earlier explained to the doctor that he had fallen from his bicycle and grazed his face on the gravel path and the sore did not seem to be healing. He now found that when shaving, he often caught the sore with the razor and had great difficulty in stopping the resultant bleeding.

As the doctor examined Jim's face closely, he noticed the discoloration around the scab, also how tender it was to the touch. The doctor had no doubt about Albert's diagnosis, but felt upset at having to tell a young man in his thirties, who was also a dear friend, that he had cancer of the face. As a doctor he was aware how important it was that treatment be commenced as quickly as possible. He turned away to try to find the right words to say to help his friend and was very surprised when he heard Jim's voice say softly, "It's all right. I have known, or should I say suspected, that I had cancer for a month or so."

As the doctor was about to speak, Jim put up his hand to stop him, and said, "Truly, it's all right. I understand how it is for you, so dispense with the sympathy and tell me what Albert said we had to do about it."

"Nothing," replied the doctor. "Only that he would talk to you alone before you return to Dundee."

"Thank you my friend," said Jim.

Next day when Helen and Jim were alone, Albert came through. He told Jim of a young man in London, Rees Evans, who had achieved some wonderful results in cancer treatment by the use of herbs. Albert advised Jim to get in touch with this young man as soon as possible. Jim worked as a salesman in a gentleman's outfitters. Wages were low and travelling expensive. It was out of the question to live in London, but he did get in touch with Rees Evans and arranged to have treatment. He took his holiday and went to London.

Evans explained that complete treatment would take about ten months. As unemployment was high, Jim could not risk losing his job by staying that long, so it was agreed that he would travel to the clinic as often as he could. He was never completely cured, but for forty years he attended the clinic and the disease was held in check. Jim died at the age of seventy-three, of pneumonia.

Helen was coming up the communal stairs to the flat one day when she met her neighbour. As usual they exchanged a few words, but that day the neighbour told Helen that there had been a man around talking to local people. She herself was one who had been questioned about Helen and her mediumship.

"What do you mean?" asked Helen.

"Well, he was asking if I ever attended any of your séances and when I said I had, he asked if I was suspicious of your mediumship and if I'd ever seen any masks or material lying about. I told him where to get off. I didn't like him or his questions."

Helen stared in amazement, as the woman went on, "I looked out of my window to see where he went. Then I saw your Bella and young Mary talking to him. He took a book out of his pocket and seemed to be writing something down. Then he put his hand in his pocket and handed something to the girls."

Greatly disturbed, Helen thanked the woman for being so informative and went indoors. As soon as Henry came in, Helen told him what she had heard.

"What do you feel about this, lass?" asked Henry.

"Do you believe me when I say I think Harry Price is behind this?" commented Helen. "I think we had better talk to the girls."

Bella and Mary were called into the sitting room and asked about the meeting with the man in the street. They both readily admitted talking to him and answering his questions about Helen's work.

"What did you tell him?" asked Henry.

Bella did not answer, but Mary said, "Well, we said we saw a shop dummy and masks and white cloth and that you kept them in the bathroom."

"Why did you lie like that?" demanded Helen.

"Well, he mentioned those things and we went along with him. He must have been pleased with us for answering his questions because he gave us ten pounds."

Henry dismissed the two girls and turning to Helen he commented, "The price of Judas has gone up!"

Within a week of the episode Mary gave notice to the Duncans, saying she had found another position and wanted to leave. Later the family was informed that Mary had gone to London, all expenses paid for by a gentleman who was investigating psychic phenomena.

Although very upset by the incident, there was little or nothing Henry or Helen could do. They could not really blame Mary or Bella, who seemed to think the whole thing a poor joke. Helen cried herself to sleep in her husband's arms. She felt that something had been started which boded ill for her and her family. Her feelings of foreboding were well justified. This was just the beginning of a personal persecution by one man, which was to continue for the next twenty-two years, only ending in her passing in 1956.

Family problems were now to interfere with the work

Helen was undertaking, which meant she had to curtail her travelling to churches throughout the country. Nan contracted rheumatic fever. Henry and Helen immediately travelled to the school in Kelso, where they found their daughter very ill. As soon as she was well enough to travel, it was arranged that all the children should be brought back to Edinburgh. Nan was ill for a year, but after this she begged to be allowed to return to school locally with her brothers and sisters, because she missed the company of children she knew of her own age. Her parents agreed, but had to keep her at home again after twice having to collect her when she collapsed in the classroom. Her education could not be neglected however and it was arranged for a teacher to visit her three times a week.

All this meant that extra money had to be found. Helen had been unable to travel and earn while the child was so ill, but work had to be undertaken to pay doctors, hospital and tuition fees. She gladly accepted work at the Psychic College, Heriot Row, Edinburgh, as this meant she could be home more often. Wonderful survival evidence was given both in Edinburgh and Glasgow at this time. Mr Ernest Oaten, editor of the Spiritualist paper "Two Worlds" often arranged and attended Helen's séances in Glasgow. Both towns always insisted that all séances be held under strict test conditions.

Séances at the Psychic College, Edinburgh were often attended by the famous Fleet Street journalist Hannen Swaffer. During materialisation séances he was allowed, with the permission of the spirit control, to touch the ectoplasm. Sometimes when his friends who had passed made a spirit return, he would be allowed to shake their hands and hold long intimate conversations. He always asserted that they felt as real as any material body and the conversations were such that no one except he and his departed friends could have known of the things discussed.

The fee paid to Helen for each séance was two guineas, quite a fee for those days. Helen did not know what the sitters were charged until quite by chance one who had been thrilled by the evidence he had received, mentioned to Helen that it was worth a lot more than the ten shillings he had paid. When she thought about it and especially when she counted the number of people attending her séances, often twenty or more, she realised someone was making a great deal of profit from her work, while she was struggling to keep herself, her husband and seven children on a mere pittance, compared with the Psychic Union's gains from her services.

She was always a generous and helpful person, many times giving her services free to churches and people in need of guidance, but too poor to pay. Never a woman to accept injustice, her temper eventually got the upper hand and angry words were exchanged with the Spiritualist Union, after which she left, saying she didn't need them and would work alone from now on. The editor of "Psychic News", Maurice Barbanell, told her of the danger of working freelance and tried to persuade her to stay within the Union, so that she would be protected by the Union while she worked. However, no extra money was offered her and she refused to back down. Sadly, she and the Union parted company and each in the end was a loser. The Union lost the services of Helen's unique gifts and Helen lost the protection of the Union, which she was to need badly in the years to come.

With the loss of permanent work at the Psychic College and the Union's premises, it was necessary for Helen to find alternative work. The family moved from the flat in Edinburgh to a council estate in Craigmillar. Not long after the move, Henry again became ill. This time it was rheumatic fever and pleurisy. The local doctor, Dr Harrison, attended him throughout his illness and was responsible for his recovery. During this time Dr Harrison came to know the family well and it was not long before he became aware of Helen's generosity to others, even if she herself mended her shoes with cardboard because they were worn and she could not afford to replace them.

Dr Harrison had many poor patients. Unemployment was high in Scotland as in the rest of the British Isles at that time. Mrs Raebourn's little three-year-old boy was only one of many whom Helen helped by paying doctor, ambulance and hospital bills. In the Thirties there was no National Health Service. When a bowl was needed to wash a new baby, when a pot was required to boil water for a home confinement, Helen was approached by Dr Harrison and his requests were always granted.

When Helen herself became ill and required a hysterectomy, she pleaded with Dr Harrison to be present at the operation himself. It proceeded as scheduled at 10.00 a.m. one morning. To all present it seemed to be going well and everything appeared normal, when a voice was heard to say, "I think you have gone deep enough."

Quickly swabbing the wound, the surgeon saw that indeed he had. Another fraction and Helen would have been in serious danger. After the operation was completed and Helen had been removed to the recovery room, the doctors and the surgeon remained in the theatre, discussing the remark about the cut being deep enough. Nobody seemed to know who said it; everybody present denied having made the comment.

"I didn't say it," said the surgeon. "I thought it was you, Harrison."

"No sir," replied Dr Harrison. "I thought the voice came from above us."

"Nonsense, man. Impossible!" snapped the surgeon.

Yet Dr Harrison thought he looked oddly puzzled as he walked away.

Dr Harrison told this to Henry as they talked later of Helen's operation. Henry asked the doctor if he could describe the voice and was told it had sounded well educated, with a sort of "Oxford accent".

"Oh, I think that could have been Albert," said Henry, looking at the doctor to see his reaction. Seeing the surprised look, he continued before the doctor had a chance to ask, to explain about Helen's remarkable gifts.

Far from being sceptical, Dr Harrison said, "That explains how she always knows when I am worried about a patient and how she will tell me when things are all right, or when they are going wrong. She is certainly a remarkable woman."

From then until he went into the army at the beginning of the Second World War, the Doctor and the Duncans remained great friends. Before joining the army, he brought the new doctor to meet the family. This man, Dr Burnett, was also to be a tower of strength to Helen and a true friend to the family during the war years.

Sadly, Dr Harrison was killed in action very early in the war.

Chapter 14

Accusations of Fraud

Many requests for help came to Helen by post. One such letter was from a Miss Souls, asking if Helen could give a sitting for a friend in need of comfort. If Helen could possibly come to 22 Stafford Street to give a demonstration of materialisation she would be most grateful.

As Helen knew the address was that of the Psychic Research Centre, she had no hesitation in telling Henry to write and give the woman a date. Henry acted in the capacity of bookings secretary, as he was more organised than Helen in the aspect of maintaining a bookings diary.

Unfortunately, the date he gave to Miss Souls was one on which Helen had already accepted a booking, which she had forgotten to confirm to Henry for the diary. As soon as the mistake was discovered Henry offered to write and cancel the booking for Miss Souls. Helen replied that this would not be necessary. If the woman needed help, she felt she ought to go and asked Henry to write and explain that she would arrive later than originally promised.

Helen's booking for the day in question was in Glasgow, at the Spiritualist Church in Holland Street, run by Mrs Drysdale, a woman she knew well. Thinking a day out would be good for Lilian and because she wanted some company on the journey, Helen decided to take the twelve-year-old Lilian with her.

It was a wonderful sitting for all who attended. One person who was there told Helen later that it seemed as if Spirit was out to prove survival and everlasting life without a shadow of doubt. One remarkable materialisation at that meeting was the father of a young lady present. When he appeared, the daughter asked the materialised father, "Where is your friend?"

"Just a minute. I'll get him," replied the spirit form, returning to the cabinet.

Then Albert's voice was heard to say, "Good gracious man, you can't bring him here!"

The other spirit voice said, "I can and I will! Come along, Boy!"

The sitters were amazed to hear the sound of hooves clopping and out of the cabinet stepped the young sitter's father again, but this time leading a beautiful horse!

The spirit gentleman drew back the curtains forming the cabinet, to reveal Helen sitting in trance in an upright chair, ectoplasm from her ears, nose and mouth. He then asked his daughter, "Who is that woman sitting there?"

The daughter tried to explain that the lady sitting in the cabinet was the instrument which had helped him to manifest.

"That's a funny looking instrument!" Then he seemed to melt into the floor, taking his horse with him.

During the laughter from the sitters which followed, the room was filled with the scent of roses. Then the wife of one of the sitters manifested and told the emotional man of her continued love for him. As she left, a rose fell on to her husband's lap. Albert told him, "She returns the rose you placed in her hand as she lay in her casement." (coffin.)

The husband confirmed that this was indeed true. As the

séance ended Albert addressed Mrs Drysdale and asked her
to tell Helen to take great care that evening. Again, after his
usual "Au revoir", he repeated, "Don't forget, Mrs
Drysdale. Tell Mrs Duncan."

"Yes, yes, I will, Albert," the woman replied.

As soon as Helen came out of trance Mrs Drysdale told
her of Albert's message. She did not take it to mean a warning
about her next appointment that evening but rather
thought that as she was in a hurry to get back to Edinburgh
for the next séance, Albert was concerned that in her haste
she might have an accident.

Because time was so short, Helen decided not to take the
time to change from her séance clothes at Mrs Drysdale's,
but to travel as she was, carrying her ordinary clothes in
her travel bag. In this way she could catch an earlier train
back to Edinburgh. For some reason she felt she should go
straight home, then the urge to send Lilian home came to
her very strongly.

"I think I'll put you in a taxi," she said.

Lilian pleaded to be allowed to stay with her mother and
Helen, now feeling too tired to argue, let her stay. They
continued on their way to 22 Stafford Street and arrived
there at 8.45pm. As they alighted from the taxi they were
met by a woman who said there had been a change of venue
and the séance was to be held next door.

She then took Helen by the arm and with Lilian by her
side Helen was escorted next door to Number 24. No other
explanation was given as to why there had been a change of
plan. In fact, no word was spoken until they had entered the
house and gone up two flights of stairs. Then the woman
asked if she would take Helen's coat. Helen said No, that
was quite all right, but was there a room where Lilian could
wait for her.

"Yes, I'll see to your daughter and then I'll come back to show you where to go," was the reply.

While she waited, Helen hung her coat on a peg on the wall and placed her travel bag on the floor below her coat. The woman returned and Helen was shown into a room where the furniture had been pushed back to leave a space in the centre for four chairs. These chairs were placed facing one corner of the room, which was curtained off to form a cabinet.

"Is there anything you would like?" asked one of the ladies present.

"Just a glass of water for after the séance, thank you," said Helen.

The séance began and afterwards Helen told Henry that all she could remember was becoming aware of somebody pulling at her and shouting, "Now we have you and your so-called spirit, Peggy!"

Peggy was a child control whom Albert sometimes allowed to take over the meeting for a few minutes.

When the disturbance occurred, Helen was hardly out of trance and very dazed. She asked what was happening.

"We are calling the police because we have caught you in the act of fraud," said a woman whom Helen later knew as Miss Maule.

"Look at this," she continued, as she held up a lady's vest.

"Where did you get that?" asked Helen, getting to her feet now fully awake.

"This is your so-called Peggy and I caught you trying to push it up your clothes," screamed Miss Maule.

Helen's temper rose and she lunged at Miss Maule shouting, "You bloody liar! You bloody bitch!"

Two of the other women present pulled Helen back.

Helen knew where the vest came from. It was part of her ordinary clothes which were in her travel bag - the clothes she had not changed into in order to save time so that she could reach this woman whom she had been asked to help. Help for what? So that she could now stand there making those terrible accusations against her.

Helen sat down crying and was still crying when the police arrived. She said nothing until the police cautioned her, then she rose to her feet and turned to Miss Maule saying, "I could kill you, you liar," and took a step forward to strike her.

The police restrained her and she was taken to the police station where she was formally charged with fraud and disturbing the peace. She was informed that she could counter-charge, but she refused to do so.

It was five months before the ordeal was to end, five of the longest months the Duncans had to endure. Henry was ill again, once more contracting pleurisy and rheumatic fever, which happened whenever he got wet and he had done so when he went to the police station to bring his wife home. Nan was suffering from jaundice, which the doctor said was as a result of shock at what had happened to her mother.

All that time Helen was under terrible strain and was quite relieved when finally she was notified of the date her case was to come to trial. She began to look forward to being cleared of the dreadful charges, as she knew she had never been party of any fraud.

90

Chapter 15

On Trial

The court was crowded that Wednesday morning, 3rd May, 1933, when the charges against Helen Duncan were read.

The clear voice of Mr James Adair, the Prosecutor Fiscal, could be heard by the many journalists drawn to that Edinburgh court by the very nature of the charges. The words had such a foreign ring to those of the Duncan family who heard them...

"Victoria Helen McCrae Duncan, it is hereby charged that on January 4th and 5th, 1933, at 1 Wauchope Place and at 24 Stafford Street, Edinburgh, pretended to eight persons, four men and four women, all residing in Edinburgh, that she was a medium through whom spirits of deceased persons were openly and regularly materialised, in such a manner as to become visible to and to speak to and to converse with those present in the room with her; that if they would attend such a séance on the said January 5th at 24 Stafford Street and to pay her a fee of 10 shillings each, or a cumulo of 3 guineas, she would attend and would materialise and render visible and audible to them deceased persons; and said eight persons having attended at said place on said date and having each paid to her the sum of 10 shillings of money, she did pretend to hold a séance there and to materialise the spirits of certain deceased persons, including that of deceased child named Peggy and did pretend that what was then visible and audible in the said room was the spirit and voice of the said deceased child. The truth, as she well knew, being that what she did pretend to be said materialised spirit of said child, was in fact a woman's stockinette undervest, held and manipulated by her, to simulate the said pretended spirit and the said audible voice was the sound of her own voice; and she did appropriate to her own uses said sums, amounting in cumulo to £4 and did defraud the eight persons each of 10 shillings sterling."

Helen pleaded 'Not Guilty' to the charges.

Mr Ian A. Dickenson appeared for the defence. Mr James Adair, Prosecutor Fiscal, conducted the prosecution.

A full report of the trial was recorded in the 'Edinburgh Evening News' of that period. The purpose here is not to restate anything written, but rather to record and show the glaring inaccuracies which were obvious to all who were involved.

Miss Esson Maule was the first witness for the prosecution. She stated in answer to a question that she had known the accused for some time. This was the first lie. Miss Maule knew of Helen Duncan by having attended a séance at the Edinburgh Psychic College. She had never spoken to Helen personally. She said that arrangements were made to hold a séance at the Duncan home, which was of course untrue. The letter had arrived at the Duncan home, but the request was for a séance at 22 Stafford Street.

This fact was verified by the evidence of a defence witness, the taxi driver, William Watson, who testified that on the night in question he had taken Helen Duncan to 22 Stafford Street as requested. As he stopped, his passenger was met by a lady who took her to the house next door, to

24 Stafford Street. This he now knew to be the residence of Miss Maule.

Miss Maule said that a number of people had gathered there on 5th January. No specific number was given, although the prosecution gave the number as eight persons. Yet only three witnesses were called for the prosecution.

Helen said then and always maintained afterwards, that she was only aware of three women and one man. The room had only contained four chairs arranged in the centre of the room, all other furniture having been pushed back.

Miss Maule's testimony stated that the room was lighted by a 40 watt red bulb, with three layers of cotton around it. When questioned she insisted that this was the only illumination in the séance room. All three prosecution witnesses agreed on the lighting in the room, yet all agreed that they could clearly see Helen Duncan seated in the cabinet in the corner of the room. The corner was at least three yards from the centre, where the chairs had been arranged.

Anyone who cares to experiment with the type of lighting described in a large, completely blacked-out room will note for themselves how difficult it is to have clear vision. In fact, it is almost impossible. Yet all three witnesses testified that they could clearly see the medium in the cabinet.

Miss Maule continued, saying that a voice purporting to be that of Albert, Mrs Duncan's spirit guide, opened the séance and had conversations with the witness.

Under defence questioning Miss Maule said that as she entered the room Mrs Duncan was breathing heavily. Helen was a large woman, who had just climbed two flights of stairs. Miss Maule said that she and the other sitters could still hear the heavy breathing, even when "Albert" was speaking.

Miss Maule's evidence is worth examining. Both Helen and Lilian were taken up two flights of stairs when they arrived. On the landing at the top of the second flight, Helen asked the woman who met them - at that time she did not know Miss Maule - if there was a place for Lilian to wait. While she was waiting, she had taken off her coat and hung it on a peg on the wall, putting her handbag and travel bag on the floor. Her travel bag contained her ordinary clothes, also some small gifts of home made jam and scones given her by Mrs Drysdale. Therefore she had time to regain her breath before being shown to the séance room.

To anyone knowing anything about trance mediumship, it is well known that the medium's breathing as she goes into trance becomes laboured and continues in this way as she goes deeper into trance. It is impossible to speak normally while breathing in this way, yet Miss Maule testified that Albert held a conversation with her and remarked that she had an awful voice for singing. "If you only heard what it sounds like you would never sing again," he had said. By way of reply Miss Maule had wished Albert a 'Happy New Year'.

Other voices were heard subsequently and figures were seen. Several of them appeared to come out of the cabinet where the medium was sitting. These spirit forms held conversations with the sitters. Later came the form of Peggy, another of Mrs Duncan's spirit controls. The witness asked the spirit form to shake hands with her. When less than an arm's length from her, Miss Maule said in her evidence, she took hold of the figure and said, "Come here and let me see what you are made of." She said she then had a feeling of stretching material, which was instantly drawn out of her grasp. Although she clung tightly to it, it slipped out of her hands as though violently tugged away from her. The middle finger of her left hand caught in a hole and she felt and heard a rip quite plainly. She was satisfied that she had torn the material. She instantly drew the curtains apart and said, "I have caught you, Mrs Duncan, in fraud!"

Another sitter, said Miss Maule, then switched on the hand lamp, which flooded the room with light. This revealed "Mrs Duncan sitting in her chair cabinet, endeavouring to put a white garment up her dress." The sleeve of the garment was hanging down several inches below her dress, which was dark brown in colour. Miss Maule then identified in court a white vest, which was produced as the garment in question. She pointed to it and said, "This is Peggy. There is the hole I made when I hung on to it and tore it."

There are many unexplained anomalies. The material "slipped from her hand" . . . then it was "violently tugged from her grasp." The undervest produced for identification was a lady's sleeveless vest. Yet when describing Helen Duncan trying to push it up her dress, the witness clearly stated that the sleeves were hanging down several inches. If Peggy was a fraud, then why was no attempt made to prove that the spirits who materialised before Peggy were also fraudulent? Perhaps it was ridiculous to expect the court to believe that a woman of 22 stone, which was what Helen weighed at the time, could cover herself from head to foot in one vest in order to impersonate other materialised forms.

The witness' evidence continued:-"The accused arose and cursed and swore. When asked to show what the article was, she refused, but after pressure did undress before the lady sitters. She only agreed to do so after considerable violence."

When questioned, "What do you mean by violence?" Miss Maule said the accused swore she would kill her. "We never once touched her," she said. "She was violent in language and action. Nobody raised a finger to her and we did not even raise our voices. It was then that the police were called."

Helen did not dispute this part of Miss Maule's evidence. She said she was in trance and was brought out of it roughly by somebody pulling her. Confused, she asked what was happening. The reply of "I have caught you in fraud, Mrs Duncan" further confused her. Never slow to anger, Helen had replied, "You liar!" By this time, she said, she had recovered from her trance state. She rose to her feet and demanded to be searched, she said, which was in direct conflict with Miss Maule's statement. Miss Maule had produced the vest, at which Helen had said, "You liar! You bloody bitch, I'll kill you for this!"

To those who knew Helen well, this was what one would call a normal reaction. All who knew her were well aware of her temper and volatile nature. But those same people were also aware of how this was compensated for by the love and compassion she could also very quickly demonstrate.

Helen said she was further angered when Miss Maule said that the money charged would be handed back to the sitters.

"Why?" she had asked. "I have done nothing wrong. I am entitled to that money."

Miss Maule had replied, "Very well, Mrs Duncan. You sign this receipt and you can have the money. I will keep ten shilling for expenses."

When the police arrived and Miss Maule again accused her of fraud, Helen admitted taking a step towards her and saying, "I'll bloody kill you, you liar!"

The police officer had put his hand on her shoulder and told her to be quiet, as she was becoming hysterical and raising her voice. She was told that she herself could bring charges, but she had refused to do so.

In his cross examination of Miss Maule, Mr Dickenson for the defence asked why, "if the witness felt Mrs Duncan to be a fraud, the séance was ever arranged?"

The reply was that the séance with the accused had been arranged by a Mrs Snowden, but Miss Maule admitted that she herself had secured the majority of the sitters. She had done this because she was being continually badgered by people who wanted to experience materialisation. She had suspected Mrs Duncan for some time, but had given her the benefit of the doubt.

Despite the fact that Miss Maule said she was being "badgered", she still apparently thought it necessary to advertise in the local paper.

Mrs Snowden in her evidence stated that she had not told Helen that the séance would take place at the Psychic Research Centre at 22 Stafford Street. She denied calling at the Duncan home on 4th January to confirm the booking. When questioned by the defence counsel, she denied meeting the accused at the taxi and re-directing her to 24 Stafford Street, Miss Maule's residence. She also denied giving the name of "Miss Souls".

Two witnesses for the defence contradicted this. Mrs Sadie O'Hara, identifying herself as Helen Duncan's house-keeper, claimed that the woman now calling herself Mrs Snowden had called at the Duncan home on 4th January. She had given her name as Miss Souls and had asked for a confirmation of the booking for 5th January. Mrs O'Hara also testified that the vest produced in evidence was one she recognised as belonging to Mrs Duncan and she herself had torn this while ironing it. She had left it on top of the ironing to be mended. On the morning of 5th January Mrs Duncan had picked it up to put on, saying it would not matter for that day, as she was in such a hurry to catch the train to Glasgow.

The defence questioned the taxi driver, Mr William Watson. He stated that until the evening of 5th January 1933, Mrs Duncan was not known to him. She asked him to drive her from the railway station to the Psychic Research Centre. He had to ask her where this was and she told him it was 22 Stafford Street. He remembered this exactly, as he had to ask where the Psychic Centre was.

He testified that a lady met Mrs Duncan as she left the taxi and although he could hear them talking, he did not hear what was being said. He saw the lady take Mrs Duncan's arm and lead her to the house next door, number 24. "I thought at the time, she did say 22," he added.

The defence then called a series of witnesses. Mrs Marguerite Linck-Hutchinson, M.B., Ch.B., D.H.P., testified that she had taken part in a series of tests held in Glasgow in 1931. Her uncle, actor Graham Moffat, had suggested to her that as a doctor she might be interested in the séances. She described how at these tests Mrs Duncan had stripped herself in her presence and, completely nude, had been examined by herself and another doctor. Mrs Duncan was then allowed to dress in black garments specially provided. It was absolutely impossible that she could have hidden any material about her person. This witness was then shown the vest and asked if Mrs Duncan could have produced "Peggy" with it. She replied that it would have been impossible to produce anything like what was seen by using a garment like that.

When cross-examined by the prosecution, this witness said that she was sure the accused could not regurgitate anything like a sufficient amount of material to account for the manifestations seen. Before the test séance the accused had eaten a meal of ham and eggs and was never out of sight of the witness between the meal and the séance. If there had been any regurgitation during the test séance, the meal would have returned. In reply to the prosecution question that Mrs Duncan may have a second stomach; this medical witness stated that it was not recognised as fact that some people had a "second stomach".

The allegations of regurgitation and the theory of a second stomach had first been made by Harry Price in London in 1931, when Helen had refused to continue with a series of so-called tests.

On Thursday, 4th May crowds flocked to the court for the resumed hearing. Many who had queued for an hour could not get in. The publicity surrounding the hearing had been enormous. The court was full an hour before the case was due to be continued.

The first witness on the second day was Mr Ernest W. Oaten, then President of the International Spiritualist Federation and editor of the leading Spiritualist journal "Two Worlds".

In his evidence he stated that he had attended some 4,000 séances and participated in 18 sittings with Helen Duncan. Defence counsel Mr Dickenson asked, "In your opinion as an authority on Spiritualism, were Mrs Duncan's spirit phenomena fraudulent?"

Oaten replied, "When I was with her, I arranged most of the sittings and laid down conditions which made fraud utterly impossible without detection. The spirits were intelligences separate and distant from Mrs Duncan and were decidedly different in form and location."

The witness then told the court that he did not think the accused or anyone else could produce the voice of "Albert", which was one of the most musical voices he had ever heard. The articulation, phrasing and elocution were perfect. The witness said he had known Mrs Duncan since 1929 and would not say her vocabulary was fluent. She always spoke with a Scottish accent and Albert did not.

When questioned about trance mediums, he replied that when a medium was in trance she was easily suggestible and in certain circumstances her actions might be influenced by the sitters. The power seemed to manifest in waves. When the phenomena were actually taking place, the medium did not seem suggestible, but only in the periods between the different phenomena.

Mr Oaten then described the test conditions imposed by him in his séances with Mrs Duncan. She was always asked to strip completely and be examined by a doctor or reliable lady investigators. This was to ensure that she could not be concealing anything about her person. She would then be put in a black sack, which was tied about her neck. She would then be placed in an upright chair and be securely tied to that chair. The rope used to tie her had long ends left, which were held by two sitters. In this way, any movement by Mrs Duncan could be detected, which made fraud impossible.

Counsel then asked Mr Oaten if he had ever witnessed unsatisfactory phenomena.

"I have several times attended sittings at which the phenomena were weak," he replied. "If it is what I call a poor séance, it is difficult for the forms to be extruded from the medium to any great distance. One expects a proportion of poor séances in any series. Induced fraud is easily possible."

When questioned further on the aspect of fraud, he said he knew enough of the subject to be able to induce fraud by hypnotic control and there was a certain class of sitter who did this wilfully. He had done this experimentally scores of times. There were factors to be considered which the ordinary man in the street did not even conceive and while he was not opposed to the occasional demonstration of materialisation phenomena to the truth-seeking public, he did not consider that they were suitable phenomena for public display. Anyone who advertised in the public press for sitters (as Miss Maule had done), or held a séance without previous search of the medium was grossly incompetent.

Dr Montague Rust, of Newport, Fife, was the next witness to be sworn in. After taking the oath he said he had known Mrs Duncan for four or five years and must have sat with her 60 times. In his opinion the best phenomena were produced in a harmonious gathering.

Mr Dickenson asked, "If a sitter made a grab at what purported to be a spirit, what effect would this have on the medium?"

Dr Rust replied, "This would have a most detrimental effect. I have sat with Mrs Duncan when this has happened. The form came out and I handed it an apple. Immediately the ectoplasm flashed right back and slapped into Mrs Duncan's face. It took three quarters of an hour for her to recover. I have seen Mrs Duncan in a state of hysteria where there has been a disturbance at a sitting."

Counsel then questioned him about regurgitation, which Dr Rust replied was absolute unadulterated nonsense. He had gone to the expense of having Mrs Duncan examined by a radiologist. She was given a bismuth meal and stood before a screen. He had personally seen the substance pass down the oesophagus and into the stomach. She could not swallow hard cheesecloth when this was tried at another test.

Dr Rust continued his evidence by describing what he had seen at some of the Duncan séances. Once the ectoplasm took the form of a snake, which clung to his shoulder and lifted him right off his feet. Later it struck against the wall with tremendous force. At that particular séance there was no curtained off cabinet. One test séance, the accused was put into a sack which was tied at the neck, having previously been stripped nude and given special séance clothes. The sack was sealed with sealing wax. Tapes were attached to the sack and tied to the chair. The cabinet curtains were then closed. The voice of Albert was then heard. "Rust," he said, "What do you want tonight?"

He replied, "I want her clothes, Albert."

Within seconds one side of the curtain had opened and he could not see Mrs Duncan, who had completely de-materialised. In a few seconds her clothes were thrown into the room and Mrs Duncan re-appeared sitting in the chair, completely naked, yet still in trance. He had covered her with some of the clothing and then examined the sack. He found the knots and seal still intact. Dr Rust concluded by saying, "She is the most remarkable woman in Europe."

The stand was next taken by Mr J. B. McIndoe, President of the Spiritualist National Union. He testified that he had arranged a series of test séances with Mrs Duncan as the medium, because of suggestions made against her in London. He considered at the time that Mrs Duncan had been unfairly treated.

When questioned by the prosecution, this witness admitted that he had written an article at the end of January 1933, which gave his opinion that the accused had been detected in fraud.

Cross-examined by the defence counsel, he was asked, "Do you still hold that view today?"

"In the light of further investigation, my views are considerably modified," he replied.

Asked to elaborate on this, he stated that the view he expressed in the article was based on statements which had appeared in the newspapers, statements made by Miss

Maule and by other witnesses who had not appeared in court. Miss Maule had told him that at the close of the séance on January 5th Mrs Duncan had made a complete confession of fraud. He now knew that this statement had been proved in court to be completely false. At the time he had written the article he had not seen Mrs Duncan, although letters had been exchanged.

Three other witnesses had asserted to him that at the séance in question they had witnessed fraud. Yet these witnesses had not been produced in court to make their statements under oath. He had no fault to find with Miss Maule as a person, but anyone who advertised in newspapers for sitters for a materialisation séance, which was supposed to be a test, was unfit to arrange such séances. It was ridiculous to suggest a test sitting with a heterogeneous collection of people obtained by advertisement.

When Helen was called to give evidence she could only give her statement up to the time she went into the trance and after she was brought out of trance by being roughly shaken by the shoulder. Even during much cross-questioning by the prosecution she maintained the same evidence as before.

A verdict of "Not Proven" was given for the allegation of fraud and she was fined £10 for using bad language and disturbing the peace.

Helen and her family and friends were not happy about the "Not Proven" verdict. It was clear to them that the hand of Harry Price was behind the whole thing. It was not possible to prove his involvement, but they were able to prove to themselves that Harry Price was known to Miss Maule. The prosecution statements regarding regurgitation and a second stomach were so much like Price's allegations in London in 1931 that they felt it too much of a coincidence to be unprompted.

It appeared to be a set-up by an unseen hand. There was the man who had approached Helen's neighbours asking about her mediumship, the man bribing Bella and Mary and Mary's sudden departure to London to "help" Harry Price. There was the letter and the visit from Miss Souls, who turned out to be Mrs Snowden and the fact that Helen was too used to appointments ever to mistake the Psychic Research Centre for any other address.

Chapter 16

The Good Years

If the hopes of those seeking to bring Helen into disrepute by the court case were that she would no longer be a creditable medium, they were doomed to disappointment. In fact, the reverse happened. Suddenly she was in demand to such an extent that she found it difficult to cope. She began to intersperse her trance and materialisation séances with psychometry sittings.

One particular psychometry demonstration was for the funds of a church run by Helen's friend and a well known medium in her own right, Lily Greig. It turned out to be a memorable evening. When Helen arrived the hall was full and it was even difficult for her to reach the rostrum, as there were so many people standing in the aisles. The tumultuous applause which greeted her made her aware that those present believed in her gifts.

On the rostrum was placed a tray containing articles which had been put there by members of the audience to be psychometrised. One article she picked up led to an evidential, but somewhat amusing result. As she picked up a medallion, Helen said, "This article belongs to a gentleman and was given to him by a lady."

Here she was interrupted by a man's voice saying, "God bless you, under my chair."

This response was greeted with peals of laughter from the audience. Oh gosh, thought Helen, I've got some poor soul here who isn't right in the head. However, the years of training and development which Henry had put her through then came to her aid. Waiting for the laughter to subside, she continued, "The lady is showing me a tea caddy."

Again the same voice called out, "God bless you, under my chair."

This time there was complete silence after the remark. Helen clasped the medallion tightly and whispered, "Oh, God help me." A rush of words now came out . . . "The tea caddy has a pattern like a willow pattern around it and the lady tells me you carry her ashes in it."

Here she was interrupted again by the same man, who shouted, "God bless you, Mrs Duncan. That is absolutely true." Bending down, he took from under his chair a parcel, which he slowly unwrapped while everyone looked on in amazement. From the wrapping he produced a tea caddy such as Helen had described. He held it up for all to see and there was a spontaneous burst of applause from the audience.

The serious researchers were always interested in test séances. At one such séance attended by Dr Rust, held at the London Psychic Research Centre, "Albert" asked Rust if he would like to examine him.

"I would like to very much," was the reply.

"Come into the cabinet please and you will see all," invited Albert.

Dr Rust entered the cabinet and was there for some minutes. As he left to take his seat again, the voice of Albert said, "You can tell the others I am certainly all man."

This remark by the spirit control left the other researchers with no doubt as to what the doctor had seen and could verify. Dr Rust then thanked Albert.

All the test séances held in London are recorded in the records of the Psychic Research Union. Many were attended by Maurice Barbanell, the late editor of "Psychic News". At one such séance Helen was handcuffed, then ropes tied round her thumbs and wrists so tightly that later it was found her skin was cut. Although Helen never complained, she must have been in pain.

When Albert came through he asked, "What is it that you want us to do?"

The sitters asked if it was possible to show them any phenomena with the medium tied in such a way.

"Well, well," replied the spirit control. "What will you gentlemen think of next? Very well, we will proceed. Will you please check that Mrs Duncan is still securely tied up? Then when you have checked this, please step back close to the cabinet and count to three."

The men did as they were directed and when they had reached the count of three, Helen was standing outside the cabinet, completely free, although still in deep trance.

Albert then spoke again. "You can examine your handcuffs and padlocks to see that they are not damaged or interfered with."

The sitters then examined the padlocks and handcuffs and found them still locked and undamaged. They asked if they could be allowed to see how Spirit had done this.

"Very well," said Albert, "Re-tie Mrs Duncan and do as I say."

When all had been prepared again, Albert instructed the sitters to leave open the curtains which formed the cabinet and to arrange their seats a few feet away, but to make sure they all had a good view of Helen chained in her chair. Albert then told them to observe the medium closely and once again to count to three. As they did so, they watched Helen slowly shrink. Her head shrank until it was no larger than an orange. Then there was a clatter as the shackles fell to the floor and again Helen was standing directly in front of the cabinet, within touching distance of the five researchers. Albert was still visible to all and said, "Take Mrs Duncan to the chair, please."

Dr Rust took the still entranced Helen to an armchair. At this point Albert could no longer be seen, but his voice continued to explain what had been done. The technicalities of the explanation are on record to those interested enough to research the Psychical Research Society's archives.

It has never been clear why, if Harry Price was sincere in his investigations, he could not co-operate with men like Dr Rust, Mr McIndoe, Hannen Swaffer, Maurice Barbanell and Will Goldstein. These men realised that people like Helen Duncan and Jack Webber were rare souls who had to be taken great care of, especially during psychic experiments. The tests were conducted in a series of proper scientific investigations, which eliminate all possibility of fraud. However, at all times the medium was convinced of their sincerity and also of the care taken to ensure that no physical or mental harm would come to the medium by any of the methods used. Experienced as they were in the investigation of psychic phenomena, they were aware of the danger to the medium from any sudden movement, bright lights, or loud noise.

However, when spirit control gave permission for photographs or a torch examination of spirit forms, these were always successful and the medium suffered no harm.

The years passed quickly. One regret that Helen and Henry had was that because of the travelling and the spirit work involved, the children grew up so quickly between their visits. Bella, the eldest, had acted as housekeeper when

Sadie O'Hara moved from the area with her family.

This arrangement worked well until Bella married and Helen and Henry felt it only fair that she, who had been such a help to them over the years, should now be allowed to devote all her time to her husband and new home.

It was important that a housekeeper be there to look after the younger children and to care properly for Nan, who had been left with a defective heart condition after a severe attack of rheumatic fever a few years previously. Accordingly, a housekeeper was engaged and Helen and Henry left sufficient money for the month before leaving to keep their previously accepted bookings. At end of the month a further supply of money was sent for the next month.

At the second week of the second month, the housekeeper suddenly left, taking with her all the money and a lot of the household linen. Nan was upset and worried, yet did not like to telegraph her parents as she knew of her mother's commitment to her spiritual work and did not want to upset and hinder her by the news. She borrowed money from Bella but Bella and her husband needed what little they had. Nan was desperate. She felt there was no way in which she could manage until the first of the month when the next lot of housekeeping was due.

Spirit told Helen that something was wrong and she would not rest until Henry agreed to go home and check, while she herself continued to keep the promised appointments. The children were overjoyed to see their father and he had hardly had time to remove his coat before they were pouring out the whole story. Henry soon sorted things out and stayed at home with the children until Helen could return.

She had arranged to be at home for the birth of their first grandchild. Bella gave birth to a lovely baby girl, who was given the name Helen after her maternal grandmother. The family enjoyed this time together, but Helen and Henry knew that they could not stay for ever. Promised sittings and demonstrations had to be honoured. The problem of someone reliable to care for the family had to be resolved so that Helen could be free. Again the hand of spirit intervened and Sadie O'Hara came to visit Helen. The two women talked of past years. Sadie's husband had died of chronic alcoholism and Helen's help and friendship had been a great comfort to her. Sadie said she felt it was now her turn to help. Both her sons were grown up and had left home to make their own way. She still felt young enough at 46 to work. They arranged that Sadie would take on the job of caring for the home and children, while Helen continued in her spiritual work.

The arrangements worked well. The children knew and loved Sadie, who was a kind and caring person. Nothing was too much trouble for her. She helped the girls with their sewing, curled their hair when they were going out, laughed and dried their tears when they brought their troubles to her. Even the boys brought their broken toys for her to mend. She washed cuts, bandaged arms and legs with the same cheerful attitude. It was Sadie who continually advocated "Give and Take", who helped in soothing the quarrels. She always told the children how silly it was to quarrel because things said in anger were always hurtful.

It seemed that in Sadie there was a direct contrast to Helen's nature, where she would either erupt in anger or joy. Sadie remained calm and serene. Did spirit send her to bring this influence to the family? Although they were all happy to see Sadie re-marry and even though the children were by that time grown up, they were still sad to see her go. It had been a wonderful six years she had given them and they knew that she now deserved this second chance of happiness for herself.

Chapter 17

Warnings of War

Henry became ill again with another bout of rheumatic fever. He had been ill for two weeks when he complained of terrible pain when breathing.

On examination by the doctor it was discovered that he had developed pleurisy. He was housebound for ten months and when he was again able to go out he found the stairs to the flat difficult and tiring.

During the years since 1933, Helen had earned quite a bit of money. There were many who were critical of the charges she made for her services. Indeed, there are many today who are critical of our present day mediums charging for their services. No criticism is made of a minister of the Church of England drawing his stipend or salary; no criticism is made of the Archbishops' palaces. The salary paid to the Archbishop of Canterbury for one year's work is possibly three times the amount which a medium can hope to earn in a lifetime's service. If we were to pay by results, how many are there who would swear that the evidence of life after death given at a sitting with a reputable medium is worth more than a year's listening to the platitudes spoken from the pulpits of orthodox churches? Only when we can answer these questions honestly can we criticise our mediums for their services.

Helen had a living to make. Her husband was no longer strong enough to continue his trade; he had a full time job travelling with her and caring for her, Helen felt safe and happiest when Henry was present at her séances. Her critics always exaggerated the actual amount of money she earned. Her normal fee for a sitting was 10 shillings, the same fee which the S.N.U. churches took for the séances arranged by them. Travel and accommodation had to be paid for and the family supported. Only her family and close friends know how much of her services were given free to those in need and in the cause of Spiritualism. Many churches still thriving today owe their origins to the free demonstrations given by Helen Duncan.

As was typical of their backgrounds, neither Helen nor Henry ever worried about amassing great material wealth. They had seen too much poverty and deprivation in their own lives and in those among whom they lived to worry overmuch about tomorrow. "Enough for Today" was their motto.

Now that Henry was no longer able to negotiate the stairs at the council flat, a decision had to be made. With what savings there were, they decided to use them to purchase a bungalow. This was in the mid-Thirties and property then was not the exorbitant price it is today.

The family was very happy in the little bungalow and for a time things seemed to be going very well. Of course, the general atmosphere of pre-war tension at times invaded their lives but in the main, contentment and a loving atmosphere prevailed.

It was in this house that the children were to experience spirit phenomena at first hand. Always aware of their mother's work and accepting the survival of spirit as a fact of life, it was no surprise to them when Spirit did manifest a presence. One such occasion related to spirit healing.

Peter, the youngest of the boys, had a very bad earache. Nan, who was looking after the household when Henry and Helen were away, took the child into her bed to try and comfort him. Cuddling the little boy as he cried in pain, she whispered, "Oh, if only Mum were here, Albert could ease this pain."

She had hardly finished speaking when she saw an ash tray, which was on the dressing table lift up, then float gently to the floor. It landed right way up, spilling none of the ash which was the residue of a cigarette she had smoked before getting into bed. Peter gave a contented sigh, said, "It's all gone now," and fell asleep.

At a séance held at that time, a gentleman sitter asked Albert's permission to record the spirit manifestations and conversations. He asked Albert if there would be trouble in Europe. Albert replied that not only would there be trouble in Europe, but a World War. More civilians than armed forces would lose their lives. Italy would start the ball rolling and as it gathered momentum the whole world would eventually become involved. He also said that Britain would lose her Empire.

Helen was disturbed when told of this prediction and all she wanted to do was gather her family close about her, as if by the nature of their unity she could protect them from the storm clouds to come. Henry arranged a holiday for the whole family. The two girls, boys and their two sons-in-law were all united for two wonderful weeks.

The night before they were due to return home, Henry noticed that Helen seemed quiet and withdrawn. When asked what was wrong she looked at him and there was great sadness in her large brown eyes. Tears fell slowly down her cheeks as she said, "Hen, it's the last time we will all be together on this earth."

Chapter 18

War and Witchcraft

The Duncan family, like most families in those early war years, suffered its own share of partings and sorrow.

Bella's husband was missing at Dunkirk. For weeks the family waited for news and eventually he returned to Folkestone on one of the fishing boats which had joined in that memorable evacuation and rescue. Nan was married to a Scots Guardsman who luckily served most of the war years in London, even though he had to endure the blitz. Sadly their baby, at the time Helen's only grandson, died at the age of eighteen months, a victim of spinal meningitis. Lilian's husband, a radio operator/air gunner with the RAF, was killed in action over Norway, even before he knew his wife was expecting their second baby.

Of the boys, Henry, the oldest, served with the RAF in the Middle East before being sent to Burma. Peter saw action in the Pacific as a signalman on an aircraft carrier, HMS Formidable. Gena, the youngest and the only one with signs of psychic ability, was declared unfit for the forces because of the problem of her hand and arm. She stayed in Scotland and worked at the Edinburgh Royal Infirmary.

Helen's services were much in demand during those years when so many people needed comfort and hope which she could offer with proof of spirit survival. The travelling was both tiring and dangerous, but Helen continued with her work. One place she served regularly for five years from 1939 was the Master Temple in Portsmouth. This was a small church run by a Mr and Mrs Homer. Helen liked these people, who were sincere Spiritualists and always made her feel welcome. She would describe them to Henry as a family who helped others as best they could, living a life of "Do unto others as you would be done by". A proportion of all collections at their services and séances were always given to a charity, nobody in need of help was ever turned away from their door.

Helen spent Christmas 1943 with her husband and Gena in their little bungalow. Nan, Lilian and her family also came to stay for the festive season. Little did they know that before a month had passed their mother would be publicly humiliated and the family subjected to ridicule and scorn by the masses.

Perhaps if Gena's dream had been taken more seriously the events which were to bring open doubts to some of the leaders of the Establishment could have been avoided. Perhaps the resultant outcry against British justice could have been averted and perhaps the law on Witchcraft would never have been changed.

Perhaps . . . perhaps . . .

But no notice was taken of Gena's premonition and eventually the events, painful and humiliating though they were, took their course and within a decade advanced the cause of Spiritualism to such a degree that by 1952 the Laws pertaining to the Spiritualist belief were updated to what we know today.

From 1942 Henry had not been fit to travel with Helen. A Mrs Brown, who had been befriended by Helen when she had been ill and accused of shoplifting in Newcastle, was asked by Helen to accompany her on a visit to Portsmouth for two weeks, from January 3rd, which had been arranged with the Homers, so Helen could serve at their church.

On the night of January 1st, Gena awoke very upset from a strange dream. So upset was she that she rushed, still in her nightdress to her parents' room and begged her father to make her mother to stay at home. When they had calmed her sufficiently to speak coherently, she told them about the dream.

"Two men were chasing Mum and she fell into a river. The men pulled her out. One man said, 'We must get her out quickly, or the mud will pull her down.' Then the scene changed. There was a high stone wall and large iron gates. I was sitting on the pavement leaning with my back to the wall and crying. I felt as if my heart was breaking. I kept crying that I must get to my Mum. I must get Mummy. I was still crying this when I woke up."

Gena then said to her father, "Please don't let her go, Daddy. I had that awful dream about London. I know it was London because the men mentioned the Thames."

"I'm not going to London," said Helen. "I'm going to Portsmouth."

"I don't care. Please, Mum, just don't go," pleaded Gena.

"Now don't be a silly lass," said Henry. "It's only a state of mind. You worry too much about your mother. Now go and put the kettle on and get your mother's insulin ready."

When her mother was at home, Gena always saw to the sterilising of needles and syringe required for Helen's injections since she had become a diabetic. As she saw to the instruments she tried to calm herself by thinking maybe her father was right. Yet she could not get away from the feeling of foreboding that something would happen to her mother.

Later, as the taxi drew up outside to take her mother to

the station, Gena once more asked her not to go.

"I'll be back in a few days," said Helen.

Her eyes blinded by tears, Gena replied, "You won't, Mum."

As Helen walked quickly away to the taxi she did not know she was driving into a nightmare which lasted for nine months.

At the séance arranged by the Homers two years earlier there were many eminent people. It was attended by about sixteen sitters in addition to Mr and Mrs Homer. The materialised form of a young sailor came through and spoke to his mother. He told her that his ship, HMS Barham, had been sunk with a great loss of life.

"That can't be. I haven't been notified," exclaimed the mother.

"You will be, mother, three weeks from now," the spirit form replied before fading from sight.

So strong was the woman's belief in Helen's manifestation that she immediately checked with the Admiralty, asking for confirmation of the sinking of HMS Barham. She was most surprised to be visited by two senior Admiralty officials, who questioned her closely about where she had received her information. She told them quite openly about the séance with a medium called Helen Duncan.

Before they left, she asked them again for news of her son's ship.

"We know nothing about it, but you will be notified through the proper channels if need be," they said. This reply neither confirmed nor denied the question put to them.

As predicted in the séance, three weeks later to the day, the woman was informed by the Admiralty with deep regret that her son had been killed in action during the sinking of HMS Barham. To those of enquiring mind, it may be interesting to check, now that records of those years are no longer "Official Secrets", as to the exact date of the sinking of this ship and why no reference is made to the delay in releasing information to relatives of the men who died.

Before the first séance ended on this latest visit, Albert spoke directly to the Homers. He warned them not to admit to the séance later in the week a gentleman who would be in naval uniform. This warning either went unheeded or was forgotten, because some days later a naval lieutenant arrived and was admitted to the séance. Those present later confirmed that the manifestations that evening were of a wonderful nature. Of all ten manifestations the only spirit form not accepted was by the naval lieutenant. Time and again, a spirit form claiming to be his aunt was denied recognition. The other sitters later commented on this, but by then events had been set in motion which none of them could have foreseen.

It was an unusual occurrence for Albert to warn against certain sitters, but again he warned the Homers not to allow in three gentlemen who would apply to come the following week. They would arrive together and one of them would be in naval uniform. Albert stressed that these men meant harm to Mrs Duncan and should not be allowed to attend any of her séances.

Looking back on events, it is easy to say that the Homers should have been more vigilant. Certainly during those emotional months of early 1944, there were many who were blamed for not taking heed of Albert's warning. How could they, simple and honest people that they were, imagine that the might of the British Establishment would be so dismayed by what had apparently been leaked by the Admiralty and Secret Service, to attend a séance at a little

Spiritualist Church? The attendance was to be for the sole purpose of silencing one who, in their eyes, had access to secret war information. What chance was there for the victim?

In recent years it is obvious that nothing has changed. We have all read of the strange and devious ways the course of justice can be diverted in defence of Establishment personages. The "Blunt affair" was but one and there have been others.

At the séance on 19th January, 1944, Helen insisted upon being disrobed and examined by two independent witnesses. She had done this ever since the unproven allegations of 1933. This was completed and she re-dressed in her séance robes and in the presence of the witnesses was conducted to the cabinet in the séance room. The curtains were closed and the sitters sang the 23rd Psalm. Albert materialised and said, "Good Evening."

Suddenly a man leapt towards the cabinet, pushed Mrs Homer aside as she was directly in front of the man, in front of the cabinet. As Mrs Homer fell, he jumped over her and pulled at the ectoplasm which had started to flow from between the curtains and was now flowing back into the medium's body. Another man put the lights on and a third rushed to the door and stood there. The word "police" was heard amid the general shouting and noise which followed.

The curtains of the cabinet were roughly pulled aside and the entranced medium was seen to be slumped forward in her chair. It was later issued in evidence that she was trying to push a sheet up her dress. Amid the general confusion Mrs Brown and Mrs Homer, aware of the danger to Helen, tried to help her, but by this time they were pushed aside by police, who had entered the room.

Later Helen could only say that she did not really know what had happened until she heard herself and Mrs Brown, together with Mr and Mrs Homer, charged with Vagrancy. Mrs Brown later stated that one of the policemen pushed aside the Homers' daughter, claiming that she had pulled a sheet from his hand and concealed it. All the accused demanded to be searched and requested that the room be searched. It seemed strange then and even stranger now, that this was not done.

Helen, Mrs Brown and Mr and Mrs Homer were charged next day at Portsmouth Magistrates Court under the Vagrancy Act.

The case against Helen was put to the court by Detective Inspector Ford, who stated that the case was viewed with some concern by Chief Constable A. C. West and he asked that Helen Duncan be remanded in custody.

Helen was not legally represented at this hearing and although all defendants requested bail, with the required sureties being available, bail was refused. Helen was remanded in Holloway jail. This was the first indication that things were not what they seemed. Four people charged under the Vagrancy Act deserved the attention of the Chief Constable, when normally this charge would have proceeded under common law. They were also denied their full rights and liberties that this law provides for.

Henry travelled to London as soon as he received the telegram informing him of what had happened. Before leaving Scotland he engaged the services of Mr Joe Smith, a Dunfermline solicitor. In London it soon became apparent to the leading Spiritualists of the day that there was much more to these arrests than was being admitted by the Authorities. The Spiritualist National Union approached Henry, offering to sponsor Helen's defence and engaged Mr C. E. Loseby, a barrister, to conduct the defence. There were many, including the Duncan family, who felt he was the wrong choice, because he was young and inexperienced and also because he himself was a Spiritualist. They felt it would have been preferable to have had a more experienced man and not one connected with the Spiritualist movement, to conduct this particular case. Nevertheless, the records show that had Solomon himself conducted the case, there was no chance of justice being done. Prejudice and superstition were upheld against simplicity and truth.

The police had not expected that the Portsmouth hearing would have been defended by a barrister. They asked for an adjournment so that they too could engage Counsel. Loseby was not content with this and protested against the treatment Helen had received since her arrest. In the following extract from "The Case of Helen Duncan" his words are recorded:-

> "It is admitted that a member of the police force, acting presumably under instruction, did a physical act which endangered the body of Mrs Duncan. The next thing is that Mrs Duncan is arrested and taken to prison. She is not allowed bail and the next thing that happens is that she is charged under the Vagrancy Act.
>
> "All this is done in a case which might well have been brought forward under the Common Law postulates. All this has been done in regard to a woman who, whatever her faults, is a woman of distinguished achievements in the past and for whom sureties could easily have been found if she had been given a chance. She has therefore been humiliated, insulted and degraded quite unnecessarily."

Detective Inspector Ford said he had been asked by the Chief Constable to obtain a further remand for two weeks. He said that the police were reporting the matter to the Director of Public Prosecutions, but that there was no objection to bail. Bail was set at £50 each for two sureties, or one of £100.

The strange nature of the charge was now beginning to emerge. No bail when there was no legal representation, yet now bail was allowed. That a simple charge of Vagrancy was to be referred to the Director of Public Prosecutions was strange; yet stranger still was the charge at the resumed hearing.

A new charge of Conspiracy was introduced. When Helen heard this she fainted in the dock. The prosecution witnesses were Stanley Raymond Worth, a naval lieutenant; Surgeon Lieutenant Fowler and Police Constable Cross. The witnesses for the defence were too numerous to mention. All four defendants pleaded Not Guilty, but the Establishment wanted blood.

Maurice Barbanell published in 1945 a fully detailed record and analysis of the trials - the Portsmouth hearing and the resultant Old Bailey procedure. This book concerns Helen Duncan, the wife and mother, caught up in what seemed to her a trial of the whole Spiritualist movement. Confused and sick, both in mind and body, she felt at the time like a piece of helpless flotsam, carried on the relentless tide of emotion generated by the whole issue.

The law moved on, hearing after hearing, witness after witness. She listened to it all as though they were talking about a stranger, not she, Helen Duncan - Henry's wife, mother and comforter of Bella, Nan, Lilian, Henry and Peter. . . and young Gena's beloved Mummy. She was not this strange conspirator those legal voices intoned about. She was not the perpetrator of fraud. She was only the little spirit boy David's "Mama Duncan". Above all, she was not a witch. Dear God, what were they saying? She was no witch.

Chapter 19

The Scales of Justice

Even to the apparently un-shockable people of England in the spring of 1944, the charge of Witchcraft brought against Helen Duncan when her trial opened at the Old Bailey, was a shock.

Those who had seen their homes demolished by enemy bombs, those who were aware of their friends and relatives butchered in the gas chambers of Hitler's Germany, who had seen the might of England reduced to a pile of rubble, could have claimed to have been beyond further credulity. Yet the shock waves of this medieval charge reverberated around Great Britain and the world. In the streets, clubs, pubs and air raid shelters people kept repeating that this was 1944, not 1735. Why now, in the midst of what was known as the bloodiest war in human history, was a woman standing in the dock of the Old Bailey, accused under a law which was more than two hundred years old?

The enlightened public asked why this particular woman, Helen Duncan, from a working class Scottish back-ground, should be prosecuted, when others, more famous or well known, proclaimed the same ideas as she. Why not Air Chief Marshal Lord Dowding, who had spoken of the same things in that very town of Portsmouth two months before Helen was arrested? Why not Sir Arthur Conan Doyle, who toured the country proclaiming the same beliefs? Perhaps they should have asked Helen, who sat in the dock. She could have told them they were wasting their time. The prejudice and superstition of the orthodox Establishment had been challenged; there could be only one outcome.

They came, the rich and the famous, the poor and the grateful, to bear witness to what they had seen. Helen sat and watched it rather like one who watches a play already knowing the plot structure of the last act. Oh yes, she was grateful to her friends. At any other time she would have enjoyed the spectacle of the Prosecution Counsel John Maude's assistant, Henry Elam, being subjected to a series of subtle replies by Hannen Swaffer which, in the eyes of the world's press, reduced Elam to the status of a stumbling amateur. She could have told "Swaff" not to even try to have photographs and X-ray pictures taken of her at the test séances allowed as evidence. He would be wasting his time.

Alfred Dodd, the author, J. W. Herries, chief reporter of 'The Scotsman', well known medium Lilian Bailey, the quiet Reverend Elliot, and little Mrs Wheatcroft from Battersea . . . they came in their dozens to speak in her defence.

Sometimes she wanted to cry out at the remarks made by the judge. She heard him talk about the war and the trial being a waste of time. Silently she screamed, "The war? Do you know as much about the war as I do? I have looked at the pitiful faces of the bereaved that came in their hundreds." Had she not seen the face of her own daughter Lilian when told of her nineteen-year-old husband's death? She watched her go into a decline and spend a year in the sanatorium after having her lung collapsed to cure the tuberculosis. Were not her two sons and two sons-in-law even now caught up in an unholy war? She had a husband who had been an invalid since the last war - "the war to end all wars", they had said.

She sat and listened to that bewigged figure calling her a humbug and a charlatan, terrible names. She listened as they talked of her making money out of people's sorrow. She heard what they said about Mrs Brown, raking up the past when fifteen years previously she had been charged with shoplifting. It had been proven at the time that the woman was ill, but again this "crime" was discussed. Was this justice and had she not already paid her penalty? She heard friends, the Homers' records of their little church's accounts being read in court. They talked of her earning £100 for her trip to Portsmouth. "Oh yes," she wanted to say. "I can tell you how I spent it. I spent it on the train fares during the other weeks of the year when I earned nothing. I spent it helping Lilian and the children, to whom this great country gives the princely sum of two pounds, nine shillings a week to live on."

But Helen said none of these things. The wise men did not ask her. Her counsel requested that she be allowed to give a séance for the jury; her only defence could be this. The judge refused and what was the point anyway? If the séance was successful she would be guilty of one thing. If nothing happened, she would be guilty of another.

As the voices droned on and the reporters of the world press listened incredulously to the mockery which purported to be British justice, Helen thought with dread of returning to prison. During the time she had spent on remand in Holloway she had been treated very badly. On one occasion when she complained that the water in her bath was too hot, the wardress had thrown a bucket of cold water over her.

Then came the voice of the judge. . . "In the case of Mrs Duncan, it is she who made the most of this and the sentence I impose upon her is nine months." Only then did

Helen call out, "I didn't do anything! Oh God . . . is there a God?" The date was the 3rd April, 1944.

Then the process of the law again came into disrepute. Mr Loseby asked for leave to appeal against all four sentences - Helen Duncan's nine months, Mrs Brown's four months and the Homers' binding over for two years. The Homers' sentence was nothing compared with their embarrassment when the trial disclosed that in fact they were not married. Unnecessary suffering was caused by the fact that "Mrs Homer" was revealed as not being a real wife and she was charged as Elizabeth Jones, even though they had lived together for more than twenty-five years. In the moral climate of those days such behaviour was thought totally shocking and did little to enlist sympathy.

Leave to appeal was so long being granted that it provided much press comment and letters to newspapers. One such letter printed in 'The Leader' said, "Ivor Novello, the actor convicted of conspiracy in connection with wartime motor car restrictions, gets eight weeks. He is allowed bail pending an appeal. Mrs Helen Duncan, the Spiritualist charged under the ancient Witchcraft Act, gets nine months and she is refused bail pending an appeal. Is there any law which governs the granting of bail in criminal cases?"

'The Solicitor', a legal journal, printed an article which contained the following:-

"It is the highest degree understandable that the credulous public should be at the mercy of credible quacks, but if it be postulated that such as a genuine Medium can exist, it is equally undesirable that such a person should be at the mercy of any person who has paid to attend a séance and who afterwards chooses to lodge a complaint for the purpose of setting in motion Section 4 of The Witchcraft Act, 1735. There is a problem here, which this conviction has not fully disposed of."

A letter from L. R. Russell, superintendent of police in the C.I.D. of Bihar, India, a province with a population of 36 million, stated:

"England has seemingly returned to the Dark Ages. In the so-called 'land of the free', Government and the police have nothing better to do than persecute modern Spiritualist mediums as 'witches'. Even in this more backward country, the Indian penal code drafted a century ago under the guidance of Lord Macauley, makes no provision for the prosecution of a 'witch'. And yet England has the face to talk of British justice and hold out its constitution as a model for the democracy of the world."

The appeal was finally heard on 8th June. For two days Helen again listened to the three judges, Lord Chief Justice Caldicote, Mr Justice Oliver and Mr Justice Birkett, argue the question of The Witchcraft Act. The court was crowded with so many reference books that there was hardly room for even one extra piece of paper. Helen heard herself compared with "The Woman Endor" and of course the New Testament had to be consulted. Had not the Lord Chief Justice strong connections with the Church of England? He was a member of the legislative committee of the House of Laity. Mr Justice Oliver had represented the Bishop of Norwich in the prosecution of the Rector of Stiffkey. Mr Justice Birkett had in his youth been a local preacher. This then was the Establishment's choice of three unbiased Judges to hear an appeal, the reason for which had been the decided bias shown during a seven day trial. What chance impartiality? What chance justice?

The judgement of the appeal court was given in an air raid shelter, as the Law Courts had been bombed. The judgement upheld the conviction. How could anyone have thought otherwise? The request for leave to appeal to the House was taken to the House of Lords. The Attorney General, Sir Donald Somerville refused on the grounds that the matter was not of public importance.

Before Helen had finished her sentence, the Spiritualist National Union, together with other Spiritualist organisations, launched a Freedom Fund, the aim of which was to modernise the law and rid their members of the threat posed by the iniquitous Witchcraft and Vagrancy Act. Seven days after Helen's release from prison, the committee of the Freedom Fund issued the following declaration:

"We have been entrusted with the task of doing everything possible to secure justice for mediums and seek the aid of all persons interested in justice and honour of British justice. Helen Duncan, in the month of March 1944, was charged under the Witchcraft Act, 1735, at the central criminal court and upon 3rd April, 1944 was convicted and sentenced to nine months' imprisonment. We are satisfied that Helen Duncan, like those charged with her, was completely innocent of the pretending brought against her, that her trial violated elementary principles of justice and she was wrongly convicted.

"In the course of her trial Helen Duncan wished to give evidence which she believed and we believe, to be final and conclusive, that she had not pretended to be a Medium, but that she is a Medium. She wished further to tender the evidence of experienced and expert persons to the same effect, but she was not allowed to do so.

"Helen Duncan was charged under an Act which is antiquated and obsolete. In the course of the case, rules relating to procedure and evidence were all laid down which, in our view, render inevitable the conviction of any innocent similarly placed.

Helen Duncan was released from prison on Friday, 22nd September and announced that she was not willing to offer her services again as a Medium to any person, whether purporting to act for scientific or religious purpose, or any other purpose."*

"Materialisation Mediums of the kind and type of Helen Duncan are very rare. Her decision constituted a grave blow to investigation, advance and progress. For the reason given above we are unable to advise Helen Duncan to offer her services again. We are aware that she would be exposed to the attack of any unscrupulous person and that, although innocent, she would in the event of an attack be convicted and still further degraded.

In this our first declaration, we wish only to make it plain our view that the condition of things above revealed is intolerable."

When the family went to meet Helen, as they travelled across London to catch the train which would take them back to Scotland, they passed the Old Bailey. All of them wondered if it had only been the flying bomb which had been responsible for the statue of Justice dropping her scales.

---

*'The Case of Helen Duncan' by Maurice Barbanell.

Chapter 20

Coming Home

Little did Helen think in that autumn of 1944 that within a year of her own homecoming, there would be many more elsewhere. The war was still very real to her as she sat in the train speeding north from London.

She was tired and ill and the journey seemed to take so long. Her thoughts went back to the spring and the nightmare she had endured. The trees had been green when the journey south to the trial had begun, the spring bulbs showing bravely through the still cold earth. Now the leaves were golden and already beginning to fall. The fields, then green with the promise of summer crops, were now brown, the corn harvested and gathered in.

"Well, mine has been a bitter harvest," she thought. "I served, I loved, I believed in justice. Will I ever be able to believe in anything again?"

Prison had not been as bad as she had imagined because she had spent most of her sentence in the prison hospital. Her health had deteriorated badly, but her past experience of ordinary hospitals had done nothing to prepare her for the bossy and sometimes brutal treatment in a prison hospital.

The family at home were overjoyed that their mother was back again. Bella and Nan came as often as they could to talk and cheer their mother. They brought the children, who had grown so much while she had been away. Lilian had moved back home to look after Henry while Gena, who was only seventeen, was at work at the hospital. Henry was so moved at Helen's return that he never wanted her out of his sight. Sometimes while she was sleeping in the afternoons he would sit by her side and often when Lilian or Gena looked in they would notice silent tears slip down their father's cheeks as he watched the sleeping Helen. They both knew their father had suffered during the trial and afterwards. So often he had said, "I never imagined this could happen when I patiently sat with her all those years to develop her gifts. If I had not done that, she would not have had to go through all this."

He himself had been humiliated while Helen was away. When she was sent to prison the Psychic College had arranged to pay him £3 per week to help the family finances. One week he had been too ill to go and collect the money. He asked Gena to go instead. Gena returned in a very angry state and when she told her father what had happened the family vowed never to go again, even if they were starving. Fuming, she told her father that she had been kept waiting around as if she were a beggar. Eventually she was called in and on being handed the money they asked her if her father had got a job. As she went to answer, one of them said, "Don't you think your mother has kept him for long enough?"

Because of this, the family never again asked for or accepted anything from the Psychic College. Henry told the girls that when they were too young to remember, their mother had served the college well for a fee of £2-2 shillings, yet the college made £8-8 shillings for every séance she gave and she gave many.

In the months which followed, Helen gradually grew

stronger. Friends came to visit and she talked of her dear
friend Jean Beatson who had visited her each week while
she was in prison. Jean would bring a bunch of violets and
hidden in the flowers she put a packet of cigarettes. Helen
said that if prison had taught her anything it was how to be
deceitful, as the cigarettes were never found. Helen also
spoke of one particular wardress who always came to her
when air raids were in progress and the flying bombs were
falling. Helen felt tired, but ill as she was, she was a source
of comfort to this woman who seemed so strong and
self-possessed.

They talked a lot in the Duncan household as the winter
passed and the spring of 1945 released the world from the
grip of war. Helen had missed so much of the girls' teenage
years because of her constant travelling. Perhaps it was for
this reason that she enjoyed so much the company of Gena,
who at eighteen was fast changing from girl to young
woman. Lilian was busy with her children, but often joined
in the many and varied conversations. Helen told them of
her childhood in Callander, the village as it was then and
the people. She told of the First World War, of her
meeting and loving Henry. The worry and strain of the
past year was uppermost in the minds of all the family and
the talking about it seemed to ease and bury the pain.

Gradually the neighbours came to ask for help and
comfort from Helen and her gifts. When she looked at the
naked misery in the faces of those she knew who had lost
sons, husbands, lovers, she just could not refuse to help.
Mothers had lost whole families; children had come home
to bombed houses. How could she not once again bring
them the comfort of knowing "There is no death", just a
brief parting between two worlds? Spiritual work again
became a normal practice in the Duncan household, but as
yet Helen would not go anywhere else. Friends came and

there were again intimate gatherings as in the early days. There were also the stupid requests which would anger Helen. One woman came regularly to the house to ask her for a winner at Powder Hall greyhound track.

Heart sore, Helen would say, "What do these silly people think mediums are for? Yes, we can help. Spirit is there to advise, comfort, console. If the need is great, sometimes advice properly interpreted can help financially. But material riches of this world are not the riches of Spirit. Spirit teaches about the richness of knowledge and advancement to the higher levels of consciousness. These are the only benefits we can take when we pass from this side of life into the next."

Helen would continually talk to her children about living a responsible life. She was always telling them to listen to the inner voice before taking any action - to stop, think and listen. If all was well the small inner voice would tell. Other advice to the family was never to speak in anger, as words spoken can never be taken back and rarely can the gap caused by hurtful words, spoken in angry haste, be bridged. Gena was reminded of the time when as a child, with a friend she had taken two shillings from her mother's purse to go to the pictures. She and Bridie had a lovely time, as there was enough for the tickets and some sweets. When she returned home Sadie O'Hara opened the door and told her that her mother wished to see her in the sitting room. As the little girl boldly walked into the room, her mother sat at the table in the centre of which lay her purse. In a quiet voice her mother said, "You know Gena that every-thing you do is noted." She was never to forget the hurt in her mother's big brown eyes and was so ashamed she could only hang her head.

The grown up Gena could now understand what her mother meant. Always there was Spirit watching over us and even if no mortal eyes see the wrongs we do, nevertheless we know what we do and our spirit friends know of it.

As Gena was the only one of her children to show signs of psychic gifts, Helen encouraged her to develop. Lily Greig, Helen's friend and herself a medium, asked Helen's permission to start a development circle at the Duncan home. Helen, always willing to help others and the cause of spiritual advancement, agreed that this could be arranged. The circle was held on Thursdays in the room which was also used for Helen's sittings. Lily borrowed the trumpet used in the early development of Helen in the hope of getting good results. The circle had been going for some months, though those sitting showed signs of developing clairvoyantly, there was no direct voice from the trumpet. Lily asked Helen if she would be kind enough to join the circle one Thursday and judge whether she thought there was any advancement.

No sooner had Helen sat down than the trumpet started to vibrate slowly, then rose in the air and went from one sitter to another, stopping at Lily. For some moments it hung suspended over her head and then dropped to her lap. A voice was then heard to say, "Hello, Ma." Lily recognised the voice as that of her son, who had been killed in a motor cycle accident some years before. After a long conversation with his mother, in which he described his progression on the other side of life, he greeted some of the other sitters whom he had known on earth. There were also other spirit voices heard as they greeted their loved ones. Then amid the excitement of the communication of spirit the more sombre voice of Albert Stewart came through to explain to Lily and the other sitters that there was no one among them who had the gift of physical mediumship. They must realise that the ability for this phenomenon was very rare indeed, but they must also not think they had wasted their time in the development circle. As they sat together in love, this love had been used by Spirit to help others, both in the spirit world and on the earth plain. Also they must realise that they had gained in friendship and joy just by being together. They had put their feet on the bottom rung of the ladder on the way to a greater understanding and spiritual knowledge. "Remember," he said, "It is by your deeds you will be known. You are responsible for your own spiritual advancement. Love one another as the Divine Force loves you. There is no cry for help that goes unheeded, or that is not answered. Remember He above gives what is needed, not what is wanted. The Divine Force sees all and can see much further than mortal eye."

No one who heard those words from Albert Stewart at the impromptu séance could ever forget them. Gena, the youngest present, was much impressed and indeed has carried those words in her heart ever since. It helps her to remember at difficult times in her own life, the simple truth and logic of those teachings.

The circle was disbanded after this, as Lily Greig had really only been interested in developing a physical medium. She was a wonderful warm-hearted woman, who continued in her work of service until her passing into spirit in 1982 as the age of 82. At Helen's passing she was a pillar of strength to the Duncan family and a true and much loved friend.

In 1945 the homecoming from all over Europe and elsewhere really began. Trains were crowded with the men and boys returning in the "demob" suits. Helen's two boys came home, but sadly neither had escaped unscathed. Henry had contracted amoebic dysentery and spent the first year of his long awaited return to civilian life in the Tropical Disease ward of the Edinburgh Eastern General Hospital.

Peter's injuries were of the mind, a result of extreme shock. This happened when a Japanese Kamikaze pilot crashed his plane on the deck of the aircraft carrier on which Peter was serving, H.M.S. Formidable and killed his best friend. For years Peter would suddenly cry out, "They're coming! Oh, God, they're coming down!" It took prolonged treatment before he was completely cured.

At about this time Maurice Barbanell's book "The Case of Helen Duncan" was published. In a way the family welcomed the book as they felt it stated the case for their mother's Old Bailey trial in a much fairer way than the reports which had been published in the press. However there were some facts he had wrong, especially about her early life. Her psychic ability had been greatly suppressed by her parents and it was not until she met and married Henry that she had developed her mediumship. At Callander there had always been upsets and misgivings. The family of a master builder, a J.P. and respected citizen of the community did not want one of his children talking to dead people! In fact, the family business is still carried on today by his grandson, Peter MacFarlane. The first stirring of development began with the first circle, when Henry and Helen lived at Arbroath, but the real progress was made when they moved to Ferry Road, Dundee.

Helen felt that the subject of her monetary reward had been falsely represented. She knew that she had never charged more to anyone than the Spiritualist National Union charged. True, she did receive all the ten shillings per person she charged when she no longer worked for the Union but the sitters had still paid the same. The only difference was that no one was making anything out of her gifts except herself. She always had to be the family's main breadwinner since Henry's heart attack. No one but she knew of the many poor people she had helped at no charge at all. It was her family who reminded her of the money she had spent on the needs of friends and neighbours, paying doctors, buying food and clothes for needy children. Helen did not even like to talk of what she did for people. "Charity without love is no charity," she would say. Her motto for life, as she would continually tell the family, was summed up in the words of a popular song: "If I can help somebody as I pass along, then my living has not been in vain."

The family and close friends had always felt that her trial had been not one of the Law against an individual, but rather the State against Spiritualism. Her close friends had advised her to retain a barrister who had no connection with the Spiritualist Movement. Helen, aware of the financial implications of such a decision, agreed that if the Spiritualist National Union was to sponsor her defence, their choice of barrister would be acceptable. Maurice Barbanell launched an appeal through 'Psychic News', but the response was so poor it had to be abandoned. To anyone who reads his book it appears obvious that the trial was indeed a trial of the whole question of Spiritualist belief and practice and the guilt of Helen as an individual was immaterial. Although the family felt very bitter about this, Helen in her patient forgiving way would say, "It probably had to be. There are certain things laid out for us and we must face them whether in this world or the next."

It was inevitable that the publicity generated by the publication of this book resulted in further pleas for Helen to resume working. More and more people came to the house asking for private sittings and eventually she consented to do some public work, but only in Edinburgh and Glasgow. Wonderful evidence was received and it would be impossible in one book to document even a quarter of it. At one Edinburgh séance a small negro boy came through and put his little hand on a gentleman's knee.

They had a long conversation in Swahili. After the séance Mr Buttle, the gentleman concerned, told us that this spirit was the son of one of the workers on his farm in Africa, who had passed into Spirit at only seven years of age. He said that the evidence he had received had given him irrefutable proof of life after death.

On one of her journeys to Glasgow Helen had another brush with fate. She had a booking for an evening demonstration at Holland Street. Nan and Lilian had arranged to meet her from the five o'clock train and accompany her. The two girls had spent the day on a shopping trip. Little Dawn, Lilian's eldest daughter, was so upset at being left behind by her mother that Helen suggested that Henry should come with her to Glasgow to give their little grandchild the treat of a train ride. When they arrived at Waverley station Henry was surprised when Helen turned to him and said suddenly, "Please take Dawn back home."

"But why?" asked Henry. "You said you'd promised to take her."

"I don't know," replied Helen. "It's just a feeling that she'll be safer with you at home."

Henry complied, as he knew better than to ignore Helen's "feelings".

As she went through the barrier Helen noticed there was no brake van, normally at the rear of the train. She knew most of the station staff by name because of her frequent journeys.

"What, no brake van?" she called to the guard. "Too bad if we hit anything."

"Oh, away with you lass, we'll be all right," was his cheery reply.

The young boy who sold sweets and cigarettes came up to

her and asked, "Would you like your cigarettes, Mrs Duncan?"

"I don't have any change, son," she answered.

"That's all right. I'll get it next time," the boy replied.

As she looked at him she again had that strange feeling she had experienced when she told Henry to take Dawn home. "No, son, I'll leave it for now."

Turning, she stepped on the train.

It was rather full and she had to make her way to the front coach, directly behind the engine. In the compartment with her were a lady and gentleman and two soldiers, one British and the other a Canadian. It did not take Helen long to start a conversation with the soldiers, telling them of her own sons and son-in-law. The time passed quickly and when she asked the time she was surprised when the Canadian said, "Five to five."

"Oh, five minutes to Queen Street, I'll go and wash my hands." (Queen Street is the main line station in Glasgow.)

When she reached the toilet it was engaged. She carried on to the next coach, where that toilet was also in use. Deciding to wait until arrival, she turned to retrace her steps when she heard a voice say, "Next coach, quick!" Helen swung round and hurried to the third coach, where she went into the toilet, placed her bag on the floor and turned to lock the door. There was an almighty bang and the next thing she was aware of was broken woodwork. She was lying upside down and there was a gaping hole where the window should have been and a large hand was tearing at the splintered woodwork. A man's voice called out, "Is anyone in there?" Helen managed to gasp, "Yes. Please help me," before losing consciousness.

Nan and Lilian, who had been waiting to meet their mother from the train, were shocked at the news of the crash. Anxiously they watched the injured being brought out on stretchers and were relieved to see their mother, though still unconscious, at least alive. They followed the ambulance to Glasgow Hospital, where they were allowed to stay the night with Helen, who had been saved from serious injury by the voice directing her to the third coach, which was the one with least damage. The first two coaches were completely wrecked; debris blocking two main lines and most of the passengers killed or badly maimed.

At home, Henry tried to calm Gena when she seemed full of tension, anxious and uneasy one minute and very excited the next.

"Dad, could there be anything wrong with Mum?" she kept asking.

Remembering Gena's premonition before her mother had left for Portsmouth and the subsequent events which were so traumatic, Henry was worried.

"I hope not, lass," he replied. "But if anything had happened to Mum, Nan or Lilian would have let us know by now."

As it was only seven o'clock Henry thought the séance would just have started and he was not expecting his family home much before ten-thirty. Gena became increasingly agitated as the evening wore on, complaining of a bad headache and nausea. These were the exact symptoms her mother was experiencing as a result of shock, but this did not become evident until the police arrived to inform them of the train crash. Helen was kept in hospital for a few days before being allowed home, where she rested for a few weeks. Yet even at home resting, she saw and gave help to many who continually came to her door. The responsibility of her unique gift was again becoming the driving force of her life.

Chapter 21

Back on the Treadmill

Like all parents before and since, Helen and Henry found that suddenly from having a house full of children, the home was now just a visiting place for a group of new families. Having known the love and close family feeling that both of them had always instilled in their children, naturally these visits were frequent. However, each now had husband or wife and it was natural that the children's horizons were widened.

The boys and Gena all married in the early post-war years. Peter married the niece of one of Helen's friends and Henry married his nurse from the Tropical Disease Hospital. Gena, the youngest and also the only one of the six surviving children to continue to serve Spiritualism, was the last to marry. Spirit had a part in her meeting her husband and this spiritual influence has continued through the years of her married life.

As Gena was getting ready to meet a boy friend to got to a Saturday football match, Helen asked her why she had not brought this boy friend home to meet the family, as was the normal understanding. All the boys and girls had brought their friends home. Gena said she had not given it much thought.

"Do you know he's married, lass?" her mother asked

gently.

"Oh Mum, he's not!" Gena replied. She quickly closed the door and left.

Helen's words had come at the correct time. That very day Gena's boy friend did not turn up for their meeting. A friend of his was passing, recognised Gena and seeing her distress he asked her what was wrong. She explained that she had a date with his friend, who had not turned up. The young man looked at her and in a very quiet voice said, "I'm sorry. But did he not tell you he was married?"

He kindly offered to escort the upset girl for the rest of the day and by the time they returned home in the evening they were such friends that Gena invited him to meet her family. What happened is an example of the influence of Spirit fitting the pieces of life's jig-saw together.

The house was in darkness when they entered. Gena walked into the dining room, followed by her new friend, George. Helen was sitting in the easy chair and Gena thought she was asleep. Because of this she told George to sit in the opposite chair, while she sat on the floor. As the room was sufficiently lit by the fire, Gena did not bother to switch on the electric light and she had hardly sat down at George's feet when the voice of "Albert" said, "Good evening Gena. Hello George, you do not know me. Gena will explain later. I knew you were coming and I have been waiting to talk to you."

What seemed strange to Gena was that George accepted this phenomenon as natural. Albert told George he had a sister in Spirit.

"No, I haven't," replied George.

"Do you not cut the grass and tend a double grave in your village?" asked Albert.

"Yes, I do," answered George.

"Is this grave not of an old lady and a little girl?"

"Why yes," replied George, surprised.

"One day you will tell me that what I have told you is indeed truth. Now Good-night and God be with you both."

When Helen came out of trance she was totally unaware of there having been a séance and after being introduced to George she left the young couple alone.

Gena explained to George that her mother was a medium and had been in trance and that the "gentleman" who had spoken to them was her spirit guide. George said he had not seen Helen sitting in the chair, but had thought they were alone. Then when the man spoke he did not know where the voice was coming from.

"You seemed to be all right," he went on, "So I knew it must be all right for me."

As they continued their conversation George told Gena that when he was sixteen he had gone with his mother to have his cards read. The lady card-reader had told him he would cross the border and would marry a girl whose parents were known the length and breadth of the country. George's home was in Shellford, Nottingham and Gena's parents were certainly known throughout the country. After investigating within his family, George was told that he did indeed have a sister, who passed to spirit when she was eight weeks old.

Gena and George were married four months after their first meeting. Both have always believed they were brought together so that they could both work for Spirit. Now, thirty-five years later George himself has travelled all Britain as a working medium and has served in the same places that Helen worked all those years ago. Spiritualism has been an ever present influence and help throughout their married life.

When their first baby was six months old, Gena was visiting her parents. She put the little girl on the bed while she spoke to her parents and a friend of her mother, Sadie Davis, a midwife from Bridgwater, Somerset. Sadie suddenly gasped in astonishment as she looked at Gena's baby. Gena looked and there on the baby's chest was the most beautiful white carnation she had ever seen. There were no flowers in the house or garden and this flower could not have been put there by any natural means. It could only have been the supernatural. This little one grew up to be a natural psychic like her father and grandmother, but because of what happened to her grandmother she wants nothing to do with Spiritualism. A sad waste of a rare gift.

With her family settled, Helen found further outlet for her maternal love of all. Into her home she took many in need of care and love, some just for a short visit, others for much longer periods. It is hard to write of Helen the medium as being separate from Helen the open-hearted woman who seemed to have the capacity to love the whole of mankind. There was a "gentleman of the road" who would call every Sunday morning. Always he was given a hot meal and a few pence. The family was instructed that even when Helen was away working, this man must always be looked after in the same way. Whenever she met anyone with some kind of handicap, Helen would say, "There but for the grace of God go I." Her family was brought up in this way and have never forgotten the lesson.

They remember the young girl from Wales who was unmarried and three months pregnant, with nobody to turn to. But when she met the Duncans she was taken in and given a loving home, cared for with her baby and eventually happily reunited with her family. Then there was Margaret, a young lass of just eighteen, whom Helen met while out shopping. The poor girl was badly afflicted with ringworm and her hair was falling out. Helen sensed the girl's heartache and in her kind way invited her and her mother to tea. There the two older women discussed the problem. Helen offered to take the girl into her home, where she could help Lilian with the chores and the children. While in the Duncan home she would receive help and healing. Helen would give her pocket money and her keep. This was wonderful for "Maggie", as she soon became affectionately known by the family. She had been unable to get any kind of job because of her disease, yet here was a stranger offering to take her into a home and family. With overwhelming gratitude she accepted.

"Oh yes, please. I was beginning to think that nobody cared," she said. "Thank you, Mrs Duncan. Thank you."

Maggie stayed four years, only eventually leaving to marry "a fine fellow" as described by Henry. During that time Helen, in addition to healing, made sure Maggie went for regular hospital treatment. When she was eventually cured, Helen bought her two wigs, as her hair had not re-grown. The two wigs ensured that Maggie need never be ashamed of her appearance while one wig was being cleaned.

The house was a happy place, always full of new and old friends. Even misfortunes were treated in a light manner. Once Jack Mackay, the medium, on a visit to Helen was telling her of the time in London when he became ill on the way to take a church service. He suffered from severe diabetes and became dizzy, starting to stagger. He held on to the railings and two people who were passing remarked, "Good God, look at that drunk!" Poor Jack, who never touched a drink, was most upset.

"Never mind, Jack," Helen replied cheerfully. "Names won't kill you. It's only shortness of breath that does that!"

Jack joined in the general laughter evoked by that

remark.

Spirit was also light-hearted in the response to some of Helen's little needs. Once during the war when cigarettes were hard to get, Helen discovered she had none. Gena offered to go and try to get some for her.

"No, never mind, lass," replied Helen. "Someone will come with some."

Gena asked if she was expecting anybody to call.

"Not really," Helen answered, smiling in a knowing way.

Shortly after this conversation the doorbell rang and when Gena answered it there stood a young woman who asked if she could see Helen in the hope of having a sitting. After the sitting was over the young woman asked Helen if she smoked. "Yes I do," said Helen.

"I'm so glad you do," said the young woman. "As you told me during the sitting, my husband is in the Navy and he sometimes brings me tins of cigarettes for friends, as neither of us smokes. I felt tonight I had to bring a tin with me when I came here. It must be intuition," she added as she handed the tin of cigarettes to Helen.

"It must be," remarked Helen. But she and Gena knew differently.

Gradually Helen took on more work. Before long she was travelling, often away from home for long weekends, then full weeks. Henry was always worried about her health. Not strong enough himself to travel with her, he knew that the dangers to his wife's health and safety were increasing every day. His fears were proved right when Helen was brought home from Alloa by friends who had arranged the sitting, Mr and Mrs Latimer. Helen was feeling very ill and had a large burn on her stomach. She went to bed immediately and agreed that Henry could call the doctor. While they waited for him to arrive, Mrs

Latimer explained to Henry what had happened. Before the séance started the Latimers had put their four-year-old son to bed and believed he was soundly asleep. When the séance had been in progress for about twenty minutes, an old gentleman had materialised to his daughter and son-in-law. He asked for a torch, "So you can really see it's me," he said to his daughter.

Mr Latimer handed a small torch to the spirit form, who then shone the light on his face asking, "Can you see me, Hen?" (An endearment used in Scotland referring to a young woman.)

"Oh yes, Dad. It is really you! Thank you for coming."

Just then there was a mighty crash of breaking glass. The spirit form immediately vanished, the ectoplasm rushed back into the cabinet and a low moan was heard from inside it. The voice of Albert called out, "Will you please see to Mrs Duncan? She's been hurt. She will be all right, but please see that she gets safely home."

When Helen was taken out of the cabinet, blood was coming from her nose and ears and her face was grey. Had it not been for the reassuring words of Albert that she would be all right, the Latimers would have believed she was dying.

Joan had sponged Helen's face and when she had recovered a little, gave her a cup of tea, then helped her to a bedroom, where she was put to rest on the bed.

"What happened?" Helen had asked.

"We don't know exactly," answered one of the women. "Joan has gone to find out."

When Joan returned she told them that her small son had got out of bed to go to the lavatory. He had been unable to open the door, so had gone to the cupboard, got a hammer and had knocked on the glass in the door, smashing it.

"Is he all right?" asked Helen, showing her usual concern for others.

"Yes, thank God. I found him hiding under the bed. When the glass smashed he had a fright. But it's you we are worried about. Are you all right?"

"I'll be fine in a little while," replied Helen.

It was while Joan was helping to remove Helen's séance clothes that she noticed the angry red weals across Helen's stomach. She turned to Henry and asked, "What could have caused them?"

Henry explained that shock and the force of the ectoplasm returning to the medium's body is not unlike an electrical burn. It can also cause internal injury and death to the medium. That is why a red light is used and sitters are asked to make no sudden noise or movement without first asking permission of the control to touch the spirit form or move towards the cabinet. This will be given, but Spirit needs a moment of time to protect the medium.

"But that spirit shone a torch on his own face," interrupted Joan. "Is that what went wrong?"

"Gracious me, no," replied Henry. "You see, when Spirit gives permission to use torches, or asks the sitter to come forward to touch or kiss their loved ones, the medium is protected. But if the movement is sudden, doing any of the things I have mentioned can have disastrous results. Up to now, Spirit have been unable to stop the instrument - that is the medium - being injured as the ectoplasm rushes back into the body:'

Joan Latimer was more upset than ever at Henry's words of explanation. Having arranged so many séances at her home, she suddenly began to realise how vulnerable are all trance mediums at the hands of inexperienced sitters. Even the accident at her home could have been avoided if she had

148

been better informed.

Helen recovered from the incident and it seemed it had caused no permanent damage. She continued with her work, mainly travelling in Scotland and just sometimes to the north of England. Within six months she had collapsed in a diabetic coma. Luckily she was at home and Henry could have her treated by the doctors who knew her medical history. Her illness continued for some time and the doctors became concerned about permanent kidney damage because of the continued high blood sugar level. Some damage had already been sustained to the kidneys because of her numerous and difficult pregnancies. She was advised by her doctor to give up her work. When she heard this, Helen looked at him and smiled her knowing smile.

"I've got to die of something," she commented. "Don't worry, Doctor."

She had always adopted this philosophical attitude when faced with ill health. She always said we all die from lack of breath and when her time came to face her Maker she would know she had done her best. This had been asked of her by Spirit in a vision she had in 1919 and she knew she would not be allowed to pass to the next world until her mission on earth was completed.

This belief gave her an inward calm and serenity which was readily apparent to all who came in contact with her. People were heard many times to remark that when she came into a room the sunshine came in with her. The family knew what was meant by this. They knew that it was a warm love for all mankind which flowered from her heart and lighted her whole being. Helen's love showed itself in practical terms. There were many times when she helped with money when her sons or sons-in-law were looking for work. Little bits and pieces to make a home comfortable in those lean post-war years found their way to each home in turn. So too did the gifts of Spirit.

Gena visited her mother and father every day and as soon as Helen was feeling strong enough after her illness she was travelling and working again, despite the doctor's warning. She was invited to Stoke-on-Trent by Gert Hamilton, who owned a little grocer's shop in Liverpool Road. In her flat above the shop she had converted one room into a séance room. In this little room some of the most evidential proof of spirit survival was given. At one sitting a young airman came to his mother. On his face was a strawberry birth mark, from his ear halfway across his cheek. A gentleman materialised, came out of the cabinet and took his wife by the hand. Two fingers were missing from his right hand. His wife confirmed positive identification and agreed when the spirit form told the sitters how he had lost his figures in a cutting machine doing his job in the printing trade. Another spirit materialised - a woman who asked for a torch. Gert, aware of the dangers, asked what the torch was for. "I want my man to see me properly," the spirit form replied.

When given the torch, the form shone it on her face. All present could see the face deformed by a hair lip. Everyone agreed that there was no way these deformities could have been faked, especially when Helen never knew who would be at any particular séance. To have "fixed" or arranged the many evidential materialisations would have required an organisation as big and efficient as the F.B.I. Helen never entered a séance room until all the participants were seated. When she came out of trance after the sitting she was given a glass of water and a cigarette, then she always left the room. Therefore she had no personal contact with the sitters.

Sometimes during a séance "Albert" would bring Helen out of the cabinet, stand beside her and ask if the sitters could see them both clearly. Albert was six feet one inch tall; Helen was five feet four inches. At other times he would open the curtains of the cabinet and ask the sitters if they could see Helen, who sat entranced, ectoplasm flowing from her mouth, nose and ears. When the sitters had confirmed what they could see, he would then show himself standing about four feet away from the medium, saying, "Now you can see us both."

There are so many alive today who can confirm this because they were there. Of course, there were occasions when the phenomena were not as clear or well formed as this. Usually this either related to the quality of the sitters, who could not generate the correct level of harmonious love necessary, or it was because the medium was not feeling well. All who have knowledge of Spiritualism are aware that in order to perform our duties properly our bodies or "instruments" as our spirit friends term them, must be in good condition. There are and were, many who have asked why Helen Duncan did not refuse to work if her health was below par. Helen Duncan above all, was aware of the hurt and disappointment of the sitters if she did not turn up for a séance. There were greedy and selfish sitters who thought only of their own satisfaction and did not give a thought for the medium's welfare.

On one particular occasion when Gena visited her mother she noticed she had a bad cold. When the sugar count was taken as Helen prepared for her insulin injection, it was too high. Gena persuaded her mother to let her telephone and cancel the evening séance which had been arranged by a Mrs Greenwood. She was amazed at the selfish reaction to her telephone call. Did she not realise that there were twelve people waiting for Mrs Duncan, asked the angry voice on the other end of the phone. It was most inconvenient for Mrs Duncan not to come. She insisted that someone would come to the Duncan home to check what Gena said about her mother being ill.

Distressed and angry that anyone could take this attitude, Gena replaced the phone and went back to check on her mother. Helen was worse, swollen from the insulin imbalance. Gena wanted to call the doctor, but Helen insisted she would be better after a cup of tea with a little sugar. As Gena was coming out of the kitchen with the cup of tea for her mother, the doorbell rang. Still with the cup in her hand, she answered the door to a gentleman who said he had come from Mrs Greenwood to take Mrs Duncan to her booking.

"I don't think so," replied Gena, "But please do come in."

When she took him into the room where Helen sat most distressed, the man was very apologetic and said he had not known Mrs Duncan was ill.

"But did you not get my message?" asked Gena. "I phoned Mrs Greenwood and explained that the reason my mother could not come was because she was so ill."

"I was simply asked if I would pick up Mrs Duncan, as I had a car and knew the district," came the reply. "But Mrs Greenwood did say that Mrs Duncan had a cold and if I came for her she might change her mind and come."

"Well, you can see for yourself that it's out of the question," said Gena, still hurt and angry that people could be so unfeeling in their treatment of her mother. Still apologising, the caller left and was not present to see that later in the evening Helen's condition so deteriorated that she suffered a heart attack. She was very ill for some weeks and the family insisted that she rest until she was fully recovered. Even when she was feeling well again they pleaded with her to take things easy and cut out the travelling to places where she had to stay overnight. Helen agreed for a time and confined her séances to those arranged by her friends, Mrs Drysdale and Lily Craig. Those good friends were interested in psychic matters and always took the greatest care in whom they allowed as sitters. Helen was thus protected from the dangers of accidents due to inexperience or ignorance of chance sitters at a trance séance.

Within a year, despite pleas from the family, particularly Henry and Gena, Helen was accepting bookings from further afield. However, they did persuade her always to take a friend to look after her. One such friend was Milly Guthrie, who lived opposite the Duncans in Rankellor Street. A booking was accepted for Dundee, when Helen told Henry that a small spot on her groin seemed to be getting larger. Henry tried to persuade her to cancel Dundee and see the doctor, but she would not agree.

"Well, if it gets worse, as soon as you come home we must have the doctor," was all the worried Henry could say.

When Helen and Milly arrived at the Johnson house in Dundee they were told that three sittings had been arranged for the week they were there. After the first séance Helen's groin was so painful that Milly insisted Mr and Mrs Johnson be told how unwell Helen was. Alex Johnson agreed that Helen should return home and he would make arrangements about the other séances arranged for the week. Too ill to argue further, Helen let Milly take her home.

As soon as they arrived Henry called the doctor, who immediately had Helen removed to hospital, where she had an operation for the removal of the abscess, which was extremely large. The incision was made from the groin to the buttock in order to facilitate the removal of the abscess core. Two pints of pus had to be removed before the core could be removed. Because she was a diabetic, Helen could not remain in the surgical ward, so she was transferred to a medical ward. A week later she complained of a dreadful pain around the wound area. When the dressing was removed it was discovered she had shingles and her physical agony was increased by mental distress of receiving a thoughtless telegram.

Two weeks after her admission to hospital, Henry and Gena found her in tears one visiting time. They asked what was wrong and Helen handed them a telegram which she had received that afternoon. Gena read from the telegram as follows: "Did you know at a moment's notice I had to fill in for you. One does not make appointments with people in spirit then cancel at last minute. Signed, Jean Thompson."

At the time, this woman was unknown to all three of them, but later she became a well known medium before passing into Spirit herself. Gena and the family often wondered if, when both women met in Spirit, Jean would have felt guilty about that ill timed and hurtful telegram. Helen's reaction was easier to imagine. Generous and forgiving throughout her stay in the world, she could only continue to love and forgive in whatever sphere she existed on. It was amazing how, throughout her life, Helen kept her faith both in the love and protection of Spirit. Bravely and humbly she accepted and faced many trials and tribulations put in her pathway through life and through her steadfastness and courage left in her family, the ability to accept and try to forgive those who had persecuted their mother. Even as she lay in that hospital bed as Gena read the telegram, she chided both Henry and Gena for their angry reaction to such an offending message.

Each illness took longer to get over, yet even before she left hospital Helen was planning for when she would work again. Mrs Roberts, a dear friend, invited her to her home in Prestatyn for a short holiday at Christmas time. Helen was still far from well and was admitted to a hospital in

Rhyl to have an insulin change. Henry asked Gena if she would go to Wales and bring her mother home. He would have gone himself, but Nan, the second daughter was also ill.

It was arranged that, on returning, a break in the journey at Stoke-on-Trent would be advisable and to stay the night with Gert Hamilton to make the trip easier for Helen. On arrival at Stoke Helen and Gena were met by a very worried looking Gert. Taking Gena by the arm and allowing Helen to walk a little ahead of them she whispered, "I have a telegram from your father. You have to phone as soon as possible and not alarm your mother."

On reaching Gert's, Gena made the excuse to phone home, saying she would just let her father know they had arrived safely in Stoke. With heart in mouth she went to the phone, knowing full well there must be something seriously wrong, otherwise her father would never have sent a telegram. Having left a husband and three young daughters at home, her thoughts were of them. Had something happened to her family? She did not expect the news she received. Henry answered the phone immediately, as though he was sitting with his hand on the receiver and as Gena said Hello her father cried out, "Oh, lass, you have to be very brave for your Mum's sake."

"What's wrong? What's happened?" she asked desperately.

"It's Nan. She passed over last night. Try and be gentle when you tell your mother. I'll meet you both in Edinburgh."

Too emotional to speak, Gena replaced the receiver and returned to Gert's place, praying she would not break down and that she would find a way to tell the awful news to her mother. Did she forget in her anguish, the power of Spirit? When she arrived at the house Helen looked at her and said, "It's all right, Hen, I know." Then they just held each other and cried.

Chapter 22

The End of the Beginning

On 30th October, 1956 Gert Hamilton alighted from a taxi outside 36 Rankellor Street, Edinburgh. As the taxi door opened, willing and worried hands helped a tired and extremely ill Helen Duncan into her own home.

In her mother's bedroom Gena helped her to undress. As she started to undress her, Helen cried out in pain.

"Oh Mum, what's wrong?" asked Gena.

"My clothes are hurting me, lass," gasped Helen.

Gena tried to be as gentle as she could in taking off the remainder of her mother's clothes, as she could see she was in terrible pain. She was relieved when she could loosen her brassiere and corsets and turned to get a nightdress which had been left ready, leaving Helen to just remove the loosened garments. She swung round when she heard Helen cry out, "Dear God, help me!" and she herself cried out in horror at the dreadful marks on her mother's body. Henry and Gert rushed in to see what was wrong.

Gena could only point to her mother and say, "Oh, look at my Mum! What have they done to her?"

There was a large burn the size of a saucer on Helen's breasts and a larger one on the abdomen. Henry took the nightdress from Gena's trembling hands and in his wonderful calming way covered Helen, telling her it would all be better soon. Continuing to talk to her as one might talk to a hurt child, he put her to bed and told Gena to get the doctor.

Within half an hour the doctor had examined Helen and told the family she would have to be taken to hospital, as she was in a state of shock.

"What are the marks on her body?" asked Henry.

"Burns," replied the doctor. "Electrical in some way."

"Could she have done this to herself?" asked Henry.

"Good God, man, there's no way she could have inflicted those upon herself. It's a wonder she's still alive."

Gena was surprised to hear her father ask those questions at such a time, but on reflection realised he would have needed to ask them if he intended to sue the police. Certainly, having heard Gert's detailed account of what happened, he was incensed at the suffering their action had caused his wife. Helen was taken to the Western Hospital where she was under treatment for a month.

She was sent home on 30th November, still ill and suffering from a vitamin deficiency which made her very depressed. That Friday afternoon the family tried every-thing, from telling jokes to talking of the fun they had had when on holiday, but nothing they said could make the smile light up on Helen's face. It was as if the spark had gone out of her; all she could do was cry.

Over the weekend she seemed to improve a little, yet when Gena arrived on Monday morning Helen was in a state of near hysteria. When Gena asked what was wrong, Helen told her to go into the bedroom to see what she had received in the post. Thinking it was another anonymous letter - there had been many - she went to fetch it. Gena smiled as she recalled one such letter: "Dear Madam, What are your spirits - whisky, gin or rum?" She certainly did not expect the type of letter she found. On the bedside cabinet was a small brown envelope on top of which was printed in bold letters NOTTINGHAM POLICE CONSTABULARY.

As Gena took the letter from the envelope and read the contents she was suddenly back in 1944. Were the police going to hound and persecute her mother all over again? The words blurred in front of her tearful eyes . . . "Madam, I have this day placed evidence before the Public Prosecutor. You will be informed of his decision at a later date." The signature was that of the Chief Constable of Nottingham.

She returned to the kitchen where her parents were sitting. Helen asked if she had read the letter.

"Yes, I have." She laughed to lighten the tension, then grew angry at the whole situation.

"What bloody evidence?" she shouted. "Don't you worry, Mum, there is nothing they can do to you."

It was impossible to describe the despair in Helen's eyes as she replied, "I could never go through another trial."

"Mum, don't do this to yourself! There is no way they can bring about a trial. There's no evidence," said Gena, fighting back her tears.

In a sort, fatalistic voice Helen said, "There was never any evidence before, but I stood accused twice."

Using all her will power to remain calm and be of strength to her mother and her sad silent father. Gena asked Henry to do the little shopping that was needed, in order to give him something else to think about and so that she could stay with her mother. At about twelve o'clock Helen asked if Henry would be much longer. Gena said he had only been gone less than an hour and he was calling in at the library to get some more books so that he could read to her. Nobody in the family ever remembered Helen reading. All their lives they could only recall Henry reading to her. Her favourites were McGonagle, the Scottish poet and McNib, who wrote verse for the 'Edinburgh Evening News'.

By twelve-thirty Helen was in so much pain that she stood pressing her clenched fist into the table and moving from one foot to the other as though she was dancing. She looked at Gena and said that if she had the courage she would take all her sleeping tablets. Gena begged her not to talk that way.

"All right, lass, I won't," said Helen. "Don't cry. I'm going to call the doctor."

Gena realised she must be in dreadful pain to talk like that. For Helen, who always had to be persuaded to see a doctor, to offer to call him herself meant she was desperate. Gena ran to phone the doctor and ran all the way back. She was relieved to find Henry had returned and together they helped Helen into bed. Henry he had bought a nice piece of lemon sole for her lunch. He cooked it and tried to tempt her to eat, as she had been unable to keep food down for the last two days.

Doctor Lugton came shortly after this and examined Helen. She told him that if only she could get rid of the pain in her back she would feel better. As Gena and Henry watched, the doctor filled a syringe from a small bottle he took from his bag. Gena asked what it was.

"Morphia," was the terse reply.

The doctor and Henry left the room together and Gena could hear them talking for some time. When Henry came back into the room he looked white and drawn. His hand trembled as he gently stroked Helen's hair and asked if she felt a little better.

"Yes," she whispered. Her eyes were glazed with the

effect of the drug. The doctor returned in the evening and then twice a day.

On Tuesday Mr and Mrs Dave Clarke came to visit their sick friend. Dave was president of Gayfield Square Spiritualist Church. Henry explained that Helen was comatose, but the Clarkes said they would sit quietly in her room for a while. Within a minute of their entering "Albert" spoke to Dave.

"I am glad you have both come, for I would like to say Good-bye," he said.

"What do you mean?" asked Dave.

Albert's voice said, "We are taking Mrs Duncan home. She has well earned her rest."

It was only weeks later that the Clarkes told the family of this experience.

On Wednesday, Henry, the eldest son came to see his mother. Helen opened her eyes and recognising Henry, asked Gena to give him the Christmas presents already wrapped in the cupboard. As Gena took them out Helen told her she had not yet bought presents for her three children.

"Don't worry about the presents now, Mum," said Henry. "I'll get them tomorrow."

"I won't be here tomorrow," said Helen. "Take them now."

As she finished speaking Gena and Henry became aware of a beautiful flower fragrance which seemed to fill the whole room. Gena gave a frightened sob, but Helen's soft voice broke in, "Don't be frightened lass. It's only my mother. And please, all of you, forgive."

She then fell into what seemed like a normal sleep. Henry left and Gena knew how upset he was. She stayed all day until the evening when she had to go home to put her children to bed. Before she left she bent to kiss her mother.

Helen's eyes opened and she said, "I love you, lass."

"Yes, I know," replied Gena.

"I don't have to ask you to take care of your father for me."

"No. I'll do that." Blinded by tears Gena went into the other room where Henry was sitting.

"I don't want to leave her, Dad. What can I do?" she said.

"Listen to me, lass," said Henry, "You must go home to your husband and children. You know your mother would worry if for one minute you neglected your family."

He got her coat and guided her to the door. Gena went home and, as if in a vacuum, attended to her family. At about midnight George, her husband, said she should go to bed, as she was so distressed she just sat in the chair, crying. He went to make her a hot drink and led her to the bedroom. As they reached the bedroom door there was a loud knock at the front door.

Gena felt her whole body go stiff as George went to open it. There was nobody there.

"Come on, my darling. It's twenty past twelve and it may be a hard day tomorrow," said George, as he returned to his wife.

At 5.30 a.m. they were awakened by another loud knocking on the front door. Gena ran to answer it and there stood a friend to say that she was to come immediately, as her father needed her.

When she arrived at her parents' house there was no need for words.

The time of Helen's passing was estimated at between midnight and 4.00 am. But Gena knew it was at twenty minutes past midnight, when a knock on her door had said, "God be with you till we meet again."

Part II

DUE PROCESS OF THE LAW

Chapter 1

"Though justice be thy plea, consider this, -
That, in the course of justice,
None of us should see salvation."

*****

If Helen Duncan sought salvation in the course of justice, she certainly did not find it. Indeed, whether her plea for justice was ever adequately answered is a matter for the individual to decide.

At the Old Bailey in 1944, nearly 40 witnesses testified that through her psychic gifts, evidence of survival after death had been proved to them. At least another 300 witnesses of her powers were prepared to give similar testimony.

Maurice Barbanell, then editor of 'Psychic News', had attended many Helen Duncan séances, often under test conditions and vouched for their genuine manifestations. He was present throughout her trial, and wrote about it in depth. He writes in his book, 'The Case of Helen Duncan' (1945):

"As I write these words there has just been released from Holloway Jail a woman who was sentenced to nine months' imprisonment because of an Act placed on the Statute Book over two centuries ago.

A few months ago I wrote a booklet, 'Rogues and Vagabonds' in which I said, 'It is the Vagrancy Act which we are determined to have amended. We do not fear the operations of the Witchcraft Act of 1735, for it is rarely invoked. Apparently the minions of the law realise that to accuse anybody of witchcraft in the 20th century might sound just a little ridiculous.'

A few days after that booklet was published, the words I have quoted were out of date. A slip had to be affixed to all copies, pointing out: '*No one could have foreseen that in the year 1944 the might and majesty of the law would be invoked to initiate a prosecution under the Witchcraft Act, 1735, as was done in the Helen Duncan case.*'"

The case of Helen Duncan began in comparative obscurity with police court proceedings in Portsmouth, after a police raid on one of her séances. The case gradually grew, more charges were added, until it eventually reached the central criminal court at the Old Bailey, by which time it had become a national talking point. Newspapers gave daily accounts of the court proceedings, with suitably eye-catching headlines such as 'SPIRIT CALLED PEGGY LIKED LIPSTICK'; 'FAIRY FORM AT SÉANCE'; 'POLICE TRAP AT SÉANCE - CONSTABLE GRABBED A SPIRIT.'

It was difficult to understand why, if Helen Duncan was a fraud, she could not have been charged under the common law of obtaining money under false pretences. This could have been dealt with locally, instead of which she was placed in the dock at the Old Bailey, charged under the Witchcraft Act.

Spiritualists believed that it all savoured of an attempt to stamp out Spiritualism because the Witchcraft Act stated that there were no psychic powers, therefore there could be no mediumship. Those claiming to be mediums were impostors, pretending to have powers which the law declared did not exist. Therefore a medium had no defence. As

Spiritualism is founded on mediumship, this law represented a grave threat to the whole Spiritualist religion.

The Vagrancy Act makes mediums "rogues and vagabonds" and the Witchcraft Act made them criminals. Not only were mediums affected, but the implications extended to members of home circles, organisers of Spiritualist meetings at which mediumship was demonstrated and even speakers on Spiritualist platforms could have been deemed guilty of contravening the Witchcraft Act, not to mention authors of books on mediumship and the editorial staffs of Spiritualist journals.

Yet it is obvious that the Witchcraft Act of 1735 was not intended to apply to Spiritualists, as Spiritualism was not known in this country until 1852, more than a century later.

Before the passing of this Act, witchcraft was legislated to be a fact. More than a century earlier, when James I was on the throne, he was prevented by rough weather in the North Sea from sailing to Denmark to bring home his bride. King James was the author of a book on demonology and because of his views an Act of Parliament was passed, imposing penalties on those who practised witchcraft. It was officially decreed that the waves of the North Sea had been made rough by witchcraft. At that time the translation of the Authorised Version of the Bible was being prepared and an attempt was made to persuade the translators to change the word "woman" to "witch" in the reference to the séance at Endor. The translators refused, but to please the king they inserted the word "witch" instead of "woman" in the italic introduction to the chapter.

In 1735 the official view of witchcraft was reversed. Previous Acts were repealed and penalties imposed on anyone pretending to exercise it. Parliament recognised that no intelligent person seriously believed in witchcraft, so the new offence became the claim or pretence to practise it. The

166

Witchcraft Act of 1735 repealed the one passed in 1603 entitled, "An Act against Conjuration, Witchcraft and dealing with evil and wicked Spirits". It also repealed an Act passed in Queen Elizabeth's reign which was "An Act against Conjuration, Enchantments and Witchcrafts".

The Witchcraft Act stated that after 24th June, 1736, "No Prosecution, Suit or Proceeding shall be commenced or carried on against any Person or Persons for Witchcraft, Sorcery, Enchantment or Conjuration, or for charging another with any such Offence in any Court whatsoever in Great Britain."

The Act was designed, it said, "for the more effectual preventing and punishing of any Pretences to such Acts of Powers . . . whereby ignorant Persons are frequently deluded and defrauded."

The penalty was clearly stated:

"If any Person shall pretend to exercise or use any kind of Witchcraft, Sorcery, Enchantment, or Conjuration, or undertake to tell Fortunes, or pretend, from his or her Skill or Knowledge in any occult or crafty Science, to discover where or in what manner any Goods or Chattels, supposed to have been stolen or lost, may be found, every Person so offending shall for every such offence, suffer Imprisonment by the Space of one whole Year without Bail or Mainprize and once in every Quarter of the said Year, in some Market Town of the proper County, upon the Market Day, there stand openly on the Pillory by the Space of One Hour."

Helen Duncan was one of the most tested mediums Spiritualism has ever produced. When she succeeded in passing one test, another was devised and demanded. Every new group of investigators, thinking there must be some flaw or oversight in previous tests, demanded more. At the time of her arrest she had been demonstrating her extraordinary psychic gifts for about twenty years. Maurice Barbanell wrote at the time:

"Helen Duncan is not a woman of any very great intellectual attainments, but she is a medium. It was not long before the physical phenomenon she obtained of materialisation - one of the rarest forms of mediumship - attracted local attention. The news spread and visitors clamoured to attend her home circle. Then she visited nearby localities and this was followed by invitations to visit towns all over the land. She was the only medium capable of demonstrating materialisation to all and sundry. So strongly had her powers developed that they seemed unaffected by her constant travelling up and down the country. This is rare, for most mediums find it necessary to confine sittings to their own home, so as to conserve the power and prevent strain."

In materialisation, what is akin to the whole process of birth is accelerated and takes place within a few minutes. The spirit form which manifests is apparently solid. It has a heartbeat; it has lungs; it can see, hear and talk. To all intents and purposes it is a living, breathing human being, albeit the manifestation is temporary. The dead who thus appear exhibit themselves as they were on earth. They are enabled to achieve this remarkable temporary appearance by a substance known as ectoplasm. The word means 'an exteriorised substance'. Ectoplasm has been chemically analysed and in one analysis by Baron Schrenk-Notzing, a German practising physician, he described it as:

"Colourless, slightly cloudy, fluid (not thready), no smell; traces of cell detritus and sputum (spittle). Deposit, whitish. Reaction: slightly alkaline."

Under the heading "Microscopic Examination" he wrote:

"Numerous skin discs; some sputum-like bodies;

numerous granulates of the mucous membrane; numerous minute particles of flesh; traces of 'sulpho-zyansaurem' potash. The dried residue weighed 8.60 gr. per litre. Three gr. of ash."

Dr W. J. Crawford, of Queen's University, Belfast, wrote a trilogy on his experiments in which he photographed ectoplasm, weighed it and traced its flow by a coloured track made from powdered carmine. By putting the medium on a weighing machine he once discovered when ectoplasm was withdrawn that she lost 54½ lbs.

Schrenk-Notzing conducted hundreds of experiments under rigid test conditions, at which in five years of sittings he took scores of photographs by a battery of cameras making simultaneous exposures. He summed up the results: "We have very often been able to establish that by an unknown process there comes from the body of the medium material, at first semi-fluid, which possesses some of the properties of a living substance, notably that of the power of change, of movement and of the assumption of definite forms."

The Baron's famous book 'Phenomena of Materialisation' contains 225 pictures of the materialisation which he had witnessed at his test séances.

Ectoplasm is a substance capable of being manipulated by spirit operators until it seems to possess all the properties of living matter. It is the basis of all physical mediumship and is used when the dead return and speak at direct-voice séances. It varies in texture and solidarity according to conditions. In its amorphous state it is usually bluey-white in appearance, self-luminous and does not reflect the red light which is habitually used at these séances. Ectoplasm has been frequently handled and pieces of it have been cut. Sir William Crookes, the famous scientist, was allowed to cut a lock of hair from a materialised form. Most of the ectoplasm used at séances comes from the medium, though a little is also collected from each sitter.

The part played by the medium in a séance is purely a passive one. The medium has no control over the phenomena, being merely the instrument of the spirit operators, from whence all the initiative and direction begins. The medium cannot conjure up the dead, or compel them to return. All that a physical medium usually does is to sit in a chair, go into trance and then awaken at the end of the séance. Usually a cabinet, consisting of the recess made by drawing a curtain across a corner of a room, is used and the medium sits behind the curtain. This is employed so that the power can be condensed and conserved.

The whole test of materialisation is in the evidence provided by the forms which build up, showing themselves in their earthly likenesses, reproducing the voice by which they were known, by familiar idiosyncrasies and by referring to incidents which establish their identity. At Helen Duncan's séances these things were vouched for on hundreds of occasions.

Maurice Barbanell comments:

"In such a unique position, Helen Duncan was confronted with two temptations. The economic law of supply and demand operated. She was always in great demand - there were always more people anxious to witness her phenomena than were capable of being accommodated. Nobody else was able to demonstrate materialisation by travelling throughout the British Isles.

The monetary temptation did arise. She may, at some time, have said to herself that she never knew when her gifts would cease to function. She may have contemplated interference at her sittings, knowing that if this occurred she might be crippled for life, or even worse. It is true to say that at every one of her sittings her life was in danger. Records tell of mediums who have been blinded and become permanent invalids because foolish sitters interfered with psychic phenomena which they did not understand."

Barbanell suggests that she may, as a canny Scot, have decided to make as much money as possible while she could, but he would not say that was necessarily the case. He warned her in 'Psychic News' on two occasions about overcharging for her sittings. He also warned her about the other temptation to which she occasionally succumbed - that of giving too many séances. Even the greatest medium has to conserve her power, because unless it is used within reason there is a drain on the physical and sensitive resources.

The question of financial reward for mediums and healers is without answer, even today. Who is to decide how much a medium should charge when dependent upon her psychic abilities for a living? The present economic system, with which and in which we all have to exist, makes it necessary for most of us to charge for our work and our talents, whether they are on a psychic level or any other level.

It is inevitable that the gift of physical mediumship brings with it the constant accusation of fraud. Almost every new witness of materialisation or other physical phenomena suspects fraud. Rumours spread and the medium is asked to undergo tests to establish authenticity. One test leads to another and Helen Duncan had more than her share. In order that there should be no opportunity for fraud in her séances she always insisted that before they took place the room, her chair and her cabinet should be examined. Two women were always present when she changed into her séance garment and she never shrank from the most intimate physical examination.

Allegations of fraud have been made from time to time against nearly every physical medium because the phenomena they have produced have been so apparently unbelievable. Naturally, there have been instances of fraudulent mediums, but although it is an easy matter to make an allegation of fraud, it is not always easy to find the proof. So was Helen Duncan exposed in fraud? Was it ever adequately proved, if proved at all?

The person who achieved greatest publicity in an attempt to expose Helen Duncan was Harry Price, who advanced the theory that her materialisations were accomplished by swallowing yards of cheesecloth, which she subsequently regurgitated. He was never able to explain how a mass of cheesecloth, taken into the stomach, could be ejected and made to look like deceased people, speak like them, often in languages and dialects unknown to the medium and do so in a way to convince their relatives and friends. Another ground for Price's allegation of fraud was that a photograph he took of the ectoplasm revealed a warp, weft and selvedge, he said. This proved that the ectoplasm was in fact a commercially manufactured cloth. It was not a theory which invoked any great enthusiasm and was considered to be very suspect.

Price's theory of regurgitation became all the more unlikely when he reported that on one occasion, under his auspices, Helen Duncan was subjected to "a gynaecological examination very thoroughly carried out". He admitted that the examination failed to disclose anything and that phenomena occurred at the subsequent séance in spite of everything.

He produced the alleged confession of a girl who had worked in Helen Duncan's household and who once accompanied her to London. When shown some photographs of ectoplasm taken by Harry Price at a Duncan séance, the girl said she recognised the tears in the cloth as being identical with those in some cheesecloth she had seen some months previously in the medium's home. In Price's report it was stated that the servant girl was "a little short-sighted", a statement which did nothing to add to the credibility of the story.

The girl's observations were published by the 'Daily Mail' and prompted a reply from J. B. McIndoe, a former president of the Spiritualists' National Union. He was one of the first to draw attention to Helen Duncan's mediumship and had attended many of her séances. McIndoe interviewed the servant girl, who, he wrote in his letter to the 'Daily Mail', had positively assured him that she had never at any time seen anything to suggest that Mrs Duncan was acting fraudulently. The 'Daily Mail' did not publish McIndoe's letter.

Not mentioned in any of Price's reports is the fact that on 23rd January, 1931, he called on Hannen Swaffer with a piece of ectoplasm which he said had been cut from Helen Duncan and had been analysed by chemical analysts. "It is the first scientific proof of the composition of ectoplasm," he told Swaffer.

In Price's presence and with his help, Swaffer dictated to his secretary a story for the 'Daily Express' for whom he was working at the time. The 'Express' did not print the story, but Swaffer's secretary recalled the incident very clearly. She placed on record how the article was dictated to her, with Price supplying the technical details, explaining what ectoplasm was and how it was formed. She remembered being shown the ectoplasm in what looked like a slide. At the time of Price's accusations of Mrs Duncan's fraudulence, Swaffer's secretary wrote, "Now I read Mr Price says it is cheesecloth. He must have forgotten."

An experiment, which was repeated many times, disposed of the regurgitation theory. Helen Duncan was asked to swallow methylene tablets, which cause the contents of the stomach to be dyed blue. After each occasion, the subsequent séance resulted in ectoplasm emerging with its usual white appearance.

Price supported his theory with another speculation that Mrs Duncan had a secondary stomach. This too was disproved by X-ray examination. Dr Montague Rust, a Scottish doctor, arranged for the medium to be X-rayed by Dr G. H. Miller of Dundee.

Dr Miller's report stated:-

"A screen examination was made of the oesophagus with the patient standing. About 15 ounces of moderately thick emulsion was swallowed and passed down a perfectly normal oesophagus at normal speed into the stomach. There is no dilatation or pouching. Examination of the stomach showed it to be of normal size, shape and position and of good normal function. There is no sign of organic disease, nor is there any departure from the normal in any way."

A medical witness who gave evidence for Helen Duncan at a previous prosecution, said: "So far from being able to regurgitate, she has a small throat. When in Dundee Royal Infirmary, it took a doctor half an hour to put a small stomach pump down her throat."

McIndoe once arranged a séance with the medium to which he invited three doctors, who later gave their verdicts on the Price theory of regurgitation. "It is the height of damned nonsense," said one, while another was even more forthright. He said, "It is an insult to the intelligence of any medical man to suggest to me that material, clean, white and with no offensive odour, came out of anyone's stomach."

A woman doctor, present at a Helen Duncan test séance, said:-

"It may interest you to know that before one of these test sittings, Mrs Duncan consumed, in my presence, a large meal of bacon and egg, with bread, tea, etc., after which she was never out of my sight until the sitting began. This makes the theory of regurgitation quite impossible and ridiculous."

In the Edinburgh Sheriff Court the principal witness for the prosecution had been a woman who stated that she seized a woman's undervest during a sitting and this garment was supposed to be a materialised form.

McIndoe, who gave evidence at the trial, stated that the evidence of this witness was almost totally different from the statements she made to him a few days after the séance which led to the prosecution. He placed it on record that in his view Mrs Duncan was wrongly convicted, an opinion shared by Scottish journalist and J.P., J. W. Herries, who repeated his opinion at the Old Bailey trial.

In all law cases involving Spiritualism, the magistrates or judges, unschooled in psychic matters, find descriptions of séances unconvincing. With all the good will in the world, their minds turn in the direction of fraud rather than believe what seems the impossible. Paradoxically, if orthodox Christians, they have no difficulty in accepting the miracles of the Bible, for which they have no evidence, but which, if presented to them in a court-room, they would reject on the grounds that it was flimsy and it too smacked of fraud!

The trial of Helen Duncan, who was described as a Spiritualist medium, began in Portsmouth Magistrates'

Court in January, 1944. She was charged under Section 4 of the Vagrancy Act which has been used repeatedly in prosecuting mediums. The section reads:-

"Every person pretending or professing to tell fortunes, or using any subtle craft, means, or device, by palmistry or otherwise, to deceive and impose on any of His Majesty's subjects . . . shall be deemed a rogue and a vagabond within the true intent and meaning of this Act."

But Helen Duncan was not charged with fortune-telling. The police used the formula coined in wartime and made her offence "the using of certain subtle means by pretending to hold communication with the spirits of deceased persons, to deceive and impose on certain of His Majesty's subjects."

The Vagrancy Act, as its title implies, was a statute designed to safeguard the illiterate and ignorant from the attention of gypsies and other vagrants. Section 4 quite clearly is directed against fortune-telling in its various forms, yet the police were able to interpolate this as they saw fit and make charges accordingly.

Spiritualists maintained that resorting to this practice was a form of sectarian bias. They are the only body of people who, as a regular practice of their religion, "hold communication with the spirits of deceased persons."

While the Witchcraft Act became law in 1735, the Vagrancy Act came into being in 1824 - both dates long before Spiritualism began, so they were never designed to be used in the prosecution of Spiritualist mediums.

Helen Duncan was refused bail at Portsmouth, although the necessary sureties were available. These were declined and the police insisted upon keeping her in prison. When proceedings were adjourned, she was taken to Holloway

Prison, in London, where she had to receive medical attention. She was a sick woman at the time, suffering from angina pectoris, valvular disease of the heart and diabetes.

When the case opened in Portsmouth, Detective-Inspector Ford said that the police had received "a number of reports of Spiritualist activities in the city."

Two months earlier, Air Chief Marshall Lord Dowding had visited Portsmouth as part of his self-imposed mission to spread the word of Spiritualism. As head of Fighter Command, he was responsible for directing the Battle of Britain. Lord Dowding told at Portsmouth how some of his young airmen had returned to him after death with proofs of their survival. Later, at the Old Bailey, one witness said she went to a Helen Duncan séance because she had heard Lord Dowding speak. Perhaps it is strange that proceedings were never instituted against Lord Dowding. Sir Oliver Lodge was not prosecuted. It was in Southsea, near Portsmouth, that Sir Arthur Conan Doyle started his investigation into Spiritualism, which led him to tour the country proclaiming his beliefs. Sir Arthur Conan Doyle was never arrested.

At the first hearing at Portsmouth, the case against Helen Duncan was outlined by Detective-Inspector Ford. He referred to meetings and séances held at The Master's Temple in Copnor Road, Portsmouth, which were advertised in the local Press. One particular meeting, which took place in a first floor room, was not so advertised.

He described the room in the corner of which was "a screen arrangement" and Mrs Duncan was the medium. There was usually an audience of about 25 or 30 people -

FORD: As a result, observations were kept and on 19th January, police officers attended a meeting. Mrs Duncan pretended to go into a trance and went behind a curtain. The lights in the room were so arranged that when this happened all lights, except a faint red one, were switched off and a spirit came on the curtain. What could be seen from the audience was a white-shrouded figure on the screen and this figure was supposed to bring messages from the spirit world. Some of the things which were divulged by the spirit were shocking and in due course evidence will be given regarding these.

Continuing his statement he said that a War Reserve policeman named Cross, dived on the figure on the screen, which was revealed to be Mrs Duncan. The white shroud with which she was covered, he said, was grasped by the police officer, but was then snatched away by a member of the audience.

It was stated in court that the Chief Constable, A. C. West, viewed the case with some concern and asked that Helen Duncan be remanded in custody. The magistrates agreed.

A deputation of Spiritualists, alarmed by this threat, visited the Home Office, but Home Secretary Herbert Morrison, refused to see them. The Spiritualists' National Union, the largest body of organised Spiritualists in the country, then instituted a Freedom Fund for the purpose of providing mediums with potential funds for legal defence. Among the deputation was a barrister, C. B. Loseby and it was he that the S.N.U. briefed for the defence of Helen Duncan.

The Portsmouth police had not anticipated such a step. When the hearing of the case was resumed, the police asked for an adjournment of the case for two weeks so that they too could be represented by counsel.

At this resumed hearing, Loseby protested against the police treatment of Helen Duncan.

LOSEBY: It is admitted that a member of the police force, acting presumably upon instruction, did a physical act which endangered the body of Mrs Duncan. The next thing that happens is that Mrs Duncan is arrested and taken to prison. She is not allowed bail. And the next thing that happens is that she is charged under Section 4 of the Vagrancy Act. All this is done in a case which might well have been brought forward under the common law, with full rights and liberties which the common law postulates. All this has been done in regard to a woman who, whatever her faults, is a woman of distinguished achievement in the past and for whom sureties could have easily been found if she had been given a chance.

(Cries of 'Hear Hear,' followed by 'Silence in court.')

LOSEBY: She has therefore been humiliated, insulted and degraded quite unnecessarily.

Detective-Inspector Ford said that he had been asked by the Chief Constable of Portsmouth to obtain a further remand of two weeks.

FORD: The matter is being reported to the Director of Public Prosecutions and the full facts are going to be placed before him for his consideration. The police have no objection to bail provided that two sureties of £50 each or one of £100 is forthcoming.

The Director of Public Prosecutions agreed to conduct the case for the police. As a result of his involvement, the next time the hearing came to court, a new charge faced Helen Duncan - one of Conspiracy.

Accused with her were Mr and Mrs E. H. Homer, who conducted the séances at the Master's Temple, Portsmouth and Mrs Frances Brown, who travelled to Portsmouth with Mrs Duncan. The new charge alleged that "between December 1943 and January 1944 she unlawfully conspired to cheat and defraud of their money such of His Majesty's liege subjects who were induced to part therewith, by falsely pretending that at so-called Spiritualist séances held at 301 Copnor Road, promoted and arranged by Ernest Edward

Hartland Homer, Elizabeth Homer, Frances Brown and Helen Duncan, the aforesaid Helen Duncan was capable of holding communication with deceased persons and causing their spirits to materialise."

When Helen Duncan heard the new charge, she stumbled from the dock, fainting. The proceedings were short and were adjourned.

At the next hearing, after all the defendants had pleaded Not Guilty, the case for the Director of Public Prosecutions was opened by J. E. Robey, son of the famous comedian George Robey.

ROBEY: This case has aroused considerable interest, but I wish to make it clear that the issue at stake is not whether there is a life after death, or whether departed spirits can communicate, or whether dead persons can materialise. The real issue is that all the defendants entered into a conspiracy by pretending that Mrs Duncan could cause the spirits of the dead to materialise.

Robey referred to the "show" put on by Mrs Duncan and the others, contrasting it with the performances of Maskelyne and Devant and said that which was done by the medium was greatly inferior.

Then he told how Worth, a naval lieutenant interested in Spiritualism, called at the Homer's shop in Copnor Road, where he was told by Mrs Homer that Helen Duncan was coming to Portsmouth to hold séances and that her ectoplasm would cause the spirits of the dead to materialise. He was warned of the danger to the medium if anyone touched the ectoplasm.

Robey summarised the events of 16th January, when Worth and Surgeon-Lt. Fowler paid 25 shillings for two tickets. The séance room was described as before - the corner cabinet, chairs arranged in a semicircle, the searching of Helen Duncan by the women and the beginning of the séance.

ROBEY: Mrs Duncan then went into what is called a trance. The only light in the room was a red one. The meeting opened with some sort of religious prayer.

LOSEBY: (interrupting) The Lord's Prayer.

ROBEY: That makes it worse. (He added that they were not passing judgement on genuine Spiritualists or on Spiritualism.)

Describing the séance attended by Worth and Fowler, Robey said that Albert, Mrs Duncan's guide, spoke in what was called an Oxford accent and Peggy, another guide, spoke in a broad Scottish accent.

ROBEY: When spirit forms appeared between - but not through - the curtains, members of the audience put leading questions, not of the 'Who are you?' kind, but 'Are you So-and-So?' One of the figures which appeared was the mutilated form of somebody who was supposed to have passed over in Singapore. After Albert had gone, Peggy spoke and sobbed. Someone asked the audience to sing and they all sang 'Loch Lomond'. Rather a puerile performance.

He told of a cat miaowing and a parrot making a noise. Then a figure of a policeman had appeared and a woman said, "Is that you, Dad?" The figure replied, "Yes. Wait till I put my helmet on."

ROBEY: After that séance Mrs Brown showed Worth some "spirit photographs", but police experts will show how these could be faked. Worth also bought tickets for another séance at 10s.6d. each. There were 20 or 30 people there and it all adds up. Mrs Duncan was giving clairvoyance and said that a little girl called Audrey had taken her by the hand. You have all heard of Little Audrey in the past! Audrey claimed a man in the audience as her father, but the man spoke up and said his daughter's name was Shirley. Mrs Duncan then apologised and said she had not heard correctly. It was after this séance that Worth informed the police.

Burrell was present at the Duncan séance on 17th January, but was asked to sit at the back. Worth was accompanied by War Reserve Constable Cross and the story was again repeated of a torch being flashed at the medium and of attempts being made to seize the spirit form. Worth shone his torch and said he saw Mrs Duncan throwing white material to the floor. It was alleged that she was frantically trying to put on her shoes.

ROBEY: It was clear that she had taken them off in order to move more easily behind the curtain.

When Mrs Duncan was asked where "the white cloth" had gone, she had replied, "It had to go somewhere."

After the séance was over, Mrs Brown had said, "Jesus suffered like this," to which Robey commented: "To trickery is added blasphemy."

At the next hearing, Lt. Worth, R.N., told how he went to the séance on 19th January, with War Reserve policeman Cross. Mrs Duncan's guide Albert appeared, as well as a figure with a baby in its arms. A young man also materialised, he said. Someone else at the séance was invited to shake hands with the figure of his dead sister. He did so and said it was a fat and clammy hand, which Worth thought "was undoubtedly human, with no etherealism or ectoplasm about it." Another time, a spirit said it was his aunt, but Worth said all his aunts were living.

The War Reserve Constable Cross gave evidence, telling how at the séance on 19th January, he had sat in the second row. Helen Duncan was the medium and both the Homers were present.

CROSS: When I saw a white shadow appear between the curtains I jumped forward towards the cabinet. As I jumped, a torch was flashed by Worth. I had previously arranged with Lt. Worth that this should be done. I clearly saw Mrs Duncan standing between the curtains clad in something white from the neck down-wards. When I reached out to take her by the arms, she was pushing the sheet downwards towards the floor. The sheet dropped to the floor and was immediately pulled towards the left of the room.

ROBEY: Did you try to get hold of the sheet?

CROSS: I laid my hands on it and actually had it in my fingers for a moment. The material was very flimsy and the nearest description I can give is that it was similar to butter-muslin. It was pulled away by someone standing on the left of the cabinet. Mrs Homer was standing near the window.

ROBEY: What happened after the cloth disappeared?

CROSS: I saw Mrs Duncan bending down, putting her shoes on. Then I told her I was a policeman and I arrested her.

ROBEY: Did Mrs Duncan ask for a doctor?

CROSS: Yes. I asked Lt. Worth if he had seen the sheet and when he replied, "No," Mrs Duncan said, "Of course it has gone. It had to go somewhere."

LOSEBY: (defence) Do you know where the sheet went?

CROSS: I don't know.

LOSEBY: Do you remember two women asking to be searched?

CROSS: I can recall one woman making this request.

LOSEBY: Why, when Detective-Inspector Ford was there, were the women not searched?

CROSS: I couldn't say. Detective-Inspector Ford was in charge.

LOSEBY: Why did you not want the women to be searched when they requested it?

CROSS: I was acting under instructions.

LOSEBY: Did the other policemen not come into the room to carry out a search?

CROSS: No.

LOSEBY: The sheet had mysteriously disappeared, yet nobody was searched for it. Did you know anything about the materialisation mediums when you went to break in, or did you make any enquiries?

CROSS: I was acting upon instructions.

LOSEBY: When you grabbed at the materialised form, did you know this was dangerous to the medium?

CROSS: No.

LOSEBY: Were you aware that it was also dangerous to flash a torch?

CROSS: No.

LOSEBY: Do you recall knocking anybody over?

CROSS: I did not knock anybody over.

LOSEBY: Did you not knock Mrs Duncan to the ground?

CROSS: I did not.

LOSEBY: Mrs Duncan fell to the ground and looked blue and distressed, did she not?

CROSS: She did not fall to the ground, neither did she look blue and distressed.

LOSEBY: But she asked for a doctor?

CROSS: Yes.

LOSEBY: Was a doctor sent for?

CROSS: I couldn't say.

Loseby wound up that part of the cross-examination by saying that Mrs Gill, one of the women present, had carried marks on her for some time after the séance.

Surgeon-Lt. Fowler told the court that he had attended a Duncan séance on 14th January, when he had felt Mrs Duncan's pulse out of curiosity, as he had been led to believe she was a sick woman. He said that after that sitting he was shown a number of photographs by Mrs Brown, who told him they were genuine spirit photographs. Towards the end of the day's hearing, a police expert in the witness-box told how he had faked similar results to those on the photographs shown by Mrs Brown.

The court then heard the evidence of Charles Robert Burrell, of Portsmouth, a dockyard worker, who told Robey that he had been a Spiritualist and medium for a number of years. He had known the Homers for about two years and towards the end of the previous summer had paid 10s.6d. for a private sitting with a medium called Redmond. He had been far from satisfied and had told Mrs Homer, at whose place the séance had been held, that he was going to report the matter to the police.

Mrs Homer, he said, told him she did not want her church to be ruined. Burrell said he had no grievance against the Homers and did not want to hurt their church at all, but he was out to stop what he called "this money racket". Mrs Homer had, in fact, returned his fee.

"For a person to pay 10s.6d. for a ten-minute conversation or communication is excessive," he said. "And that is half the fee."

Burrell told how, after his disappointing session with Redmond, he attended a Duncan séance at the Homers' place on 17th January. He sat in front of the curtain. Soon after the lights went down he saw a white shadowy form. He could not distinguish any figure it was represented to be.

Then a figure had appeared holding a torch. All torches had been collected from sitters before they went into the séance room. A hand, covered with "this cloth or misty affair", held the torch, which was claimed by a marine as his property. The spirit form - or the entity - said, "I have been through your pockets and got your torch."

Asked at the end of that séance for his opinion, Burrell said he was not convinced. Mrs Homer had said, "You, a Spiritualist, after all these years are not convinced now, when all these poor people who don't understand, are convinced?"

Burrell had said that was why they were convinced - because they didn't understand. He was invited to another séance and was told to sit or stand at the back. He heard the voice of Albert, but did not know whose voice it was. "We call him Albert," he said. A form appeared and Mrs Homer said it was that of Mrs Allen, a former member of the church who had not long passed over. Apparently Mrs Allen had something wrong with one of her arms when she died. On the figure which appeared, Burrell saw a swelling on the arm, which was more like an arm than any of the previous forms. It was a lot more solid. He had paid nothing for the two Duncan séances which he had attended.

Cross-examined by Loseby, Burrell said he was sure he was a medium - a person through whom spirits from another world communicated. Loseby repeated the question, asking Burrell if he was sure he was a medium. Burrell said he was quite sure. Asked whether he knew anything about materialisation mediums Burrell said, "Nothing whatever." He had heard of Sir William Crookes, the famous scientist who had held materialisation séances under laboratory test conditions and had read about him.

Loseby asked, "Do you know that there are such persons as materialisation mediums through whom spirits from another world communicate and who for the time being take on a material form? They use material from the medium and the sitters."

Burrell agreed with that and was then asked to name a greater medium for materialisation than Helen Duncan. He replied that the Duncan séance was the first materialisation he had attended.

"Are you in agreement with Sir William Crookes?" asked Loseby.

"On some points," came the reply.

Detective-Inspector Ford was the next witness. He told how, when he entered the room at Copnor Road, he ordered everyone present to keep their seats. Cross had informed him that he had held the cloth in his left hand, but that somebody sitting on the left of the room had snatched it away. Ford said the room was searched, but no cloth was found.

Mrs Homer's daughter Christine, who had been sitting on the window seat near the curtain, had become excited and asked to be searched. So did some of the others. Ford had asked for the cloth to be handed to him, but it was not. Nobody had been searched. Mrs Duncan had said to him, "I have nothing to worry about." She was taken into another room by a policewoman and a few minutes later her séance clothes had been handed to him.

He told how he had asked Mrs Brown - after Mrs Duncan had been taken away - to go with him and Worth into the next room, where she was questioned about the spirit photographs she had shown Worth. There was some talk about the photographs and Mrs Brown had said of Mrs Duncan that she was a medium - the only one she knew who paid income tax! This statement brought forth the first laugh in court that day.

Ford said that at the police station Mrs Duncan had said she was suffering from heart trouble and diabetes. A police surgeon had come to examine her and gave a certificate.

Loseby began his cross-examination of Ford by asking whether he realised the importance of the sheet. The inspector said he did, going on to say that a complete search had been made of the room, but not of the occupants.

LOSEBY: It must have been in the room, unless it was de-materialised, of course, or on some person in the room, or in their possession?

FORD: *Yes.*

LOSEBY: *But the women were willing to be searched. A policewoman was present and could have searched them.*

FORD: *That would have required a doctor to be present.*

LOSEBY: *I suggest you knew there was no sheet.*

FORD: *I believe otherwise.*

LOSEBY: *Do you agree with the last witness that there are such things as genuine materialisation mediums?*

FORD: *I really don't know.*

LOSEBY: *Did you know that the séance was going to be violently interrupted?*

FORD: *I knew it was going to be interrupted. I gave orders for it.*

LOSEBY: *I suggest that your orders to Cross to seize the materialised form were monstrous.*

FORD: *I do not think so, but my orders were carried out.*

LOSEBY: *Accompanied by kicks.*

FORD: *That is a matter of opinion.*

LOSEBY: *Does that answer arise out of ignorance or deliberation?*

FORD: *Deliberation.*

LOSEBY: *Accompanied by ignorance?*

FORD: *That is a matter of opinion.*

LOSEBY: *Witnesses would say that Mrs Duncan was blue in the face and distressed.*

FORD: *She was no bluer than she is in court today.*

LOSEBY: *Did a nurse accompany Mrs Duncan to the police station?*

FORD: *A midwife stayed with her for two and a half hours.*

LOSEBY: *On whose authority were Mrs Duncan's finger-*

prints taken?

FORD: That's my responsibility.

LOSEBY: Did you take fingerprints without authority?

FORD: As far as I know, the prisoner was asked. I arrived when the fingerprints were being taken.

Later answers elicited that at that time the prisoner was not legally assisted by anyone. Ford said he was not aware that while Mrs Duncan was in the city, her doctor telephoned.

Answering Robey, Ford said he was not told that, at the séance when Mrs Duncan was arrested, it was no use looking for the cloth, because it had rushed back into the medium's body.

Apart from the police expert photographer, there were two more witnesses - William Lock, of North End, Portsmouth, a licensed pedlar and his wife, who were both at the séance on 19th January. Lock said that when invited to take the hand of a spirit said to be that of his dead sister, he did so, but the supposed spirit's hand was very cold and flabby. It was a very fat hand.

Mrs Lock said she saw someone on the floor and noticed something pass through Cross's fingers. It looked like a very thin piece of material and disappeared towards the bay window. She told of another séance when white material "just disappeared through the floor," and Peggy, Mrs Duncan's child control, asked them to sing 'You Are My Sunshine'. She had paid 12s.6d. for the séance and Robey commented, "For the pleasure of this entertainment."

The long hearing took place in a curious atmosphere. The evidence was taken down by a clerk using a typewriter, overhead aircraft roared and somewhere nearby someone was playing a piano, running rapidly through dance tunes.

Chapter 2

"I charge you by the law,
Whereof you are a well-deserving pillar,
Proceed to judgement."

*****

Before the next hearing the action had moved from Portsmouth Magistrates' Court to the Old Bailey, in London, the most prominent courtroom in the country. For seven days, reporters crowded in to report the daily sensations of case which attracted world-wide attention.

During the interval between the last Portsmouth hearing and the Old Bailey trial, there were consultations between the office of the Director of Public Prosecutions and the Recorder, Sir Gerald Dodson. As a result, the Witchcraft Act was incorporated into the list of seven charges facing the defendants. Originally, the sole offence was under the Vagrancy Act. Then was added the charge of Conspiracy. Finally came the Witchcraft Act, alleging that the defendants "had pretended to exercise or use a kind of conjuration, that through the agency of Helen Duncan, spirits of deceased persons should appear to be present in such place as Helen Duncan was then in and that the said spirits were communicating with living persons there present."

Another charge under the Larceny Act was of "causing money to be paid by falsely pretending they were in a position to bring about the appearances of the spirits of deceased persons and that they then, bona fide, intended to do so without trickery." It was also charged that "they effected public mischief by holding meetings, at which people were admitted on payment, at which Mrs Duncan professed that the spirits of deceased persons were present, or visible through her agency."

During the hearing, the Recorder suggested that the charges of larceny and causing a public mischief should be dropped. This was agreed, leaving the one indictment of Conspiracy, under the Witchcraft Act. John Maude, K.C. and Henry Elam spoke for the prosecution. For the defence, counsel was C. E. Loseby and T. S. Pedler.

In an opening speech of one and a half hours, Loseby invited the wartime jury of seven, one woman and six men, to have test séances with Helen Duncan. He said the medium was willing to proffer herself to try to produce the form or voice of her spirit guide. "It is the acid test," he said. "If Mrs Duncan has a guide he will be with her now, probably trying to help her in the Central Criminal Court." He explained that all she would need was a bare room, with a small portion curtained off and a red light.

Loseby said Spiritualists welcomed the trial and it was at the express wish of the defence that the defendants were brought to the Old Bailey, because it was an opportunity long and eagerly awaited by that particular body of opinion.

"It is what they have always asked for," he said, "And it would be churlish and most dreadfully wrong if any complaint were made by one of them.

"Each of the three women and the man in the dock I believe - but I am not quite sure - are Spiritualists. I will ask the jury to say that charges under the Witchcraft Act are simply ridiculous.

"As to the allegation that Mrs Duncan used a kind of

conjuration to bring about the appearance of the spirit of a dead person, is there any evidence to say Mrs Duncan has done anything more than be a materialisation medium - a person through whom, with or against her will, certain spirits came from another world. Can the Lord's Prayer be called a conjuration? I am going to argue that the Witchcraft Act of 1735 is completely obsolete so far as this type of case is concerned."

On the charge of causing a public mischief, Loseby said, "I cannot imagine that soldiers will fight less bravely because they have been told that hope has become a certainty, that there is no such thing as death and that continuity of life can be scientifically proved. It is not a public mischief if it can be proved scientifically that the ancient philosophies of the world are true. That is the defence."

Referring to the evidence he intended to call, Loseby said, "I ask the jury to watch for references to features - a nose, eyes, or a birthmark. That cannot be done by Mrs Duncan playing bogey-bogey with a sheet over her head.

"If Mrs Duncan has a guide, he will be with her now; probably trying to help her here; possibly waiting for an opportunity to help her. If it is true, you may be sure of it - here in the Central Criminal Court. If she be a person through whom these spirits form contacts and under certain circumstances materialise, she might show them here. Why not?

"I am going to ask you, if you think it would help you, to ask the learned Recorder if you might be allowed to see - possibly you might hear, the voice of her guide - for yourself. You might be able to judge whether it was her voice or a different voice.

"I should promise nothing. But it would be a matter of comment against me if nothing happened - if you saw nothing or heard nothing. It is the acid test to which this woman ought to be willing to subject herself. She is so willing. Doctors can be present. Any proper method to prevent fraud may be adopted. It would be much better still if she were taken completely by surprise.

"In the matter of time and occasion, all that would be required would be merely a few moments in which she could tranquilise her mind. I would proffer Mrs Duncan at the right time for that purpose and under such conditions as the judge thinks right."

The Recorder's reply was, "I must leave you to conduct the case in your own way. It is much more satisfactory if you keep to the ordinary rules governing the ordinary procedures of these courts with which you are familiar and I think this is the better course to pursue."

When the Recorder suggested that Mrs Duncan should give evidence first, Loseby replied, "Mrs Duncan can give no evidence at all, her case being that she is in a trance at her séances, other than at this one point saying, 'I proffer myself' I shall proffer her. Apart from that, she is not giving evidence."

Loseby referred to two previous experiments when Mrs Duncan was interrupted in a séance by a light being suddenly flashed for the purpose of taking photographs. He said she was wounded and an "angry" mark, a burn, showed itself at the second experiment in the region of her cheek. When he later repeated his offer of séances for the jury the Recorder said, "There is no use wasting the time of the jury in witnessing some kind of demonstration. It is bad enough a London jury having to try a case from Portsmouth, without having their time occupied by witnessing exhibitions which may or may not assist them."

John Maude, for the prosecution, opened the case against Helen Duncan by saying, "This has nothing to do with witchcraft." All the defendants had pleaded Not Guilty and

Maude explained that, although people could no longer be prosecuted for witchcraft, they could be prosecuted for "pretending" they could do something like that. For example, he said, they might pretend to turn a poor village idiot into a toad and scare the whole countryside.

"This case is not aimed at the honest beliefs of any person," he said. "This prosecution is aimed at common fraud. In the reign of James I it was a popular matter to chase poor deluded creatures thought to be witches, but in time our forefathers began to think it was ridiculous to prosecute people for something which was impossible and in the reign of George II the law was altered."

He read the provisions of the Act under which the indictments were framed, adding that genuine believers in Spiritualism would no doubt warmly support any measure directed against the "fraudulent and deplorable activities of persons pretending anything such as the calling back of the dead. At this time when the dead are no doubt anxiously thought after and anxiously sought after in prayer, such conduct as to pretend to conjure them up when it is a false and hollow lie is nothing less than a public mischief"

He repeated the story of the séances at 301 Copnor Road, Portsmouth) with "the attractive title" of 'The Master's Temple', which was registered as a church, but he could see no advantage in that, except that no rates were paid. In speaking of the charge of 12s.6d he added, "That might be moderate if you were going to see the ghost of the Duke of Wellington or Napoleon, but not if you are going to see a bogus conjuring trick. If you are going to see the mutilated body of your boy, which was purported to be shown at one of these sittings, it would be horrible and painful beyond description."

The so-called ectoplasm was something like a strip of muslin or cheesecloth, or perhaps a towel. Mrs Homer had explained to the sitters that if the ectoplasm was touched it would rush back into the medium's body with such force that it might seriously injure Mrs Duncan or even kill her. In fact, the ectoplasm did not go back into her body. The suggestion of the Crown is that the towel was snatched by a confederate and disappeared.

"Three women searched Mrs Duncan before a séance in very much the same way that Maskelyne and Devant asked people to come on to the stage. On the alleged appearance of animals at these séances, one needs to get hold of one's sanity. Had the cat been interrupted while hunting pink mice in the Elysian fields?"

In reference to spirit photographs taken by Tyneside medium Thomas Lynn, which Mrs Brown showed at Portsmouth, these were faked, said Maude. A Portsmouth policeman who was a photographer would show how they were done. Mr and Mrs Homer and Mrs Brown acted as "suggesters" at Mrs Duncan's séances.

"If the prosecution's case is proved," Maude concluded, "We shall have turned on the light a bit in the little room at Portsmouth and drawn the curtains back in 'The Master's Temple' and the mockery of the dead will have ceased in the little room above Mr Homer's shop."

Junior counsel, Henry Elam opened the examination of Worth, who told for the first time of a conversation with Mrs Homer in which she had said that sometimes when the ectoplasm returned to Mrs Duncan it picked up small objects like cigarette ends and matches.

ELAM: Like a vacuum cleaner?

WORTH: Yes.

Worth again described in detail the first séance he had attended on 14th January, the opening prayer, Albert the guide who had "an Oxford accent" and the light from one red bulb.

WORTH: When a figure appeared I said, 'Are you my aunt?' and the figure replied 'Yes' in a husky voice. I said that all my aunts were living. Then I was told of a sister who was born prematurely. My only sister is living. I have attended ordinary Spiritualist meetings at The Master's Temple, but then there were no psychic phenomena demonstrated."

Worth described how Mrs Duncan's séance clothing had been examined at the sitting and said they were "thin black garments". He was satisfied there was no white material in them. Three women went into another room with Mrs Duncan and undressed her. When she returned she was wearing the garments which had been searched. The women told the sitters they were satisfied with their search.

To the amusement of the court Worth told of the animal materialisations and gave impressions of them. The name of a parrot was given as Bronco and it said, 'Pretty Polly'. A cat had miaowed and he had also heard the voice of Albert.

"When all lights except the red one were put out," said Worth, "The room was in darkness, but after a time it was possible to distinguish objects. A form inside the curtain spoke to a medium called Taylor Ineson, who said, 'Is that you, Jarvis?' A bulky figure came out and shook hands with Taylor Ineson, who was in the second row. They had a jovial sort of talk. The figure said it did not think much of the medium; she was too fat. The figure and Ineson had a private joke together and I caught the words 'bloody twisters', coming from the figure in a Yorkshire dialect."

Worth said that when Albert said he had the mutilated form of a young man killed in an explosion out East, a woman stated it was for her. She was asked to touch the stump of an arm and when Albert asked her, she said she had felt it. Worth said it could have been anything. When questioned he said that the voices from the cabinet had all been different.

"After the séance Mrs Homer asked me what I thought of it. I said it was all very amazing. Mrs Brown asked me a similar question and I told her I thought it was amazing."

On 16th January, Worth again went to The Master's Temple, paying 3 shillings for two tickets, but on the previous day, 15th January, he had gone to the police.

RECORDER: *Did you go back on your own initiative, or on police instruction?*

WORTH: *On police instruction. At that séance Mrs Duncan gave an address in what sounded like Albert's voice and Mrs Brown gave clairvoyance. After the meeting Mrs Brown stopped me at the door and asked what my doctor friend had thought of it, as he had accompanied me to the first meeting. I said, 'Don't worry about him. He believes it.'*

On 17th January, Worth saw Inspector Ford of Portsmouth police and later that day went to Copnor Road and booked two seats for a séance on 19th. He paid 25s. for the seats. This was the séance which he attended with War Reserve Constable Cross. The same search of Mrs Duncan's clothes was carried out, but this time one man asked for the Hessian to be stripped from the bottom of the chair on which Mrs Duncan sat.

When the third figure appeared, Cross pushed his chair forward and snatched at the figure, while Worth flashed his torch.

"I saw Mrs Duncan trying to get rid of about two to three yards of white material, pushing it towards the floor. The cloth disappeared towards the left. By the light of the torch I saw Mrs Duncan bending down, trying to put on her shoes. Soon after that she yelled for a doctor. Then I blew my police whistle."

Loseby began his cross-examination of Worth by asking

about his contact with Portsmouth police.

LOSEBY: Were you acting as the police's spy at Copnor Road?

WORTH: I was spying on my own account. I decided on the afternoon of the materialisation séance that I had been defrauded and I intended to satisfy myself. Before that I had gone there with an open mind.

LOSEBY: Why was it necessary to tell so many lies after 14th January? You told Mrs Homer that the séance was amazing. Did you intend to convey that it was amazingly good?

WORTH: It was stronger than that.

LOSEBY: Then what did you mean to convey?

WORTH: I intended to convey that it was just amazing.

LOSEBY: Can you explain why you said that the doctor had believed what he had seen? This was not true, surely?

WORTH: It was not true, but I said it.

When the Lock family of Portsmouth were mentioned, Lock having already appeared as a witness, Worth said he did not know them.

LOSEBY: Very frankly, I suggest that you know them quite well. Had you decided, in December 1943, to bring about the downfall of Mrs Duncan?

WORTH: In December 1943, I had an open mind about the whole business.

LOSEBY: Did you not at that time, tell the Lock family that you were going to Copnor Road as a bona fide seeker?

WORTH: I did not know any of the Locks in December 1943.

LOSEBY: It would be libellous to suggest that even before you had seen Mrs Duncan you were working in the dark for a summons to be taken out against her.

WORTH: I don't follow you.

LOSEBY: Would you be surprised to know that bets were being offered in Oxford in the first week of January 1944, that a summons would be taken out within 14 days against Mrs Duncan and that you were concerned in it?

WORTH: I would be surprised.

LOSEBY: Let us return to the séance on 14th January, when Albert told you of your sister, prematurely born. You recall your denial. The following Sunday morning you went to the meeting at Copnor Road and told Homer, 'You remember Albert requesting me to confirm the statement that I had a prematurely born sister? On Saturday I phoned my mother and she said it was true.'

WORTH: I was acting upon police instructions.

LOSEBY: Why did you tell that lie?

WORTH: I considered Mr Homer had told enough lies, so I decided to give him some of his own medicine.

LOSEBY: Did people other than yourself claim to recognise the materialisations?

WORTH: They did after being prompted. I came to the conclusion that the happenings were unspiritual.

LOSEBY: Is it true that the figure of Peggy, Mrs Duncan's child control, had a slight figure.

WORTH: (amused) I saw a bulky figure. Whenever I saw anything it was a bulky figure.

Loseby took Worth through the materialisations, figure by figure and recalled how many people had claimed them as recognisable. Worth did not agree.

LOSEBY: You thought Mrs Duncan was playing bogey-bogey with a sheet over head?

WORTH: I was sure that was what went on.

Cross-examined, Worth stated he was satisfied there was nothing fraudulent in the cabinet before the séance. Further questions revealed that Worth was 28 and had gone to the police to denounce Mrs Duncan after his first materialisation séance. He did not mention his suspicions or consult any member of the development circle to which he belonged at the Master's Temple.

On the second day of the hearing, Worth was recalled by Elam. Worth then corrected a statement he had made the previous day, when he had said he was acting upon police instructions when he lied to Homer about telephoning his mother to ascertain he had a premature sister. He now maintained that he had acted of his own free will, considering it in the interests of justice. But he did attend the séance on police instructions.

Surgeon-Lt. Elijah Fowler, who went with Worth to the first séance, said he could not get near enough to see the figure clearly, although he was in the front row in a good position. But at a distance of two feet he could distinguish outlines in the red light.

LOSEBY: Did you examine Mrs Duncan after the séance?

FOWLER: I did not examine her, but I felt her pulse.

He said he knew nothing of the scientific side of the subject. He told the Recorder that some of the figures were quite bulky and some were quite slim.

Detective-Inspector Ford, cross-examined by Loseby, was asked how he could explain the disappearance of the white sheet with which it was alleged the forms were produced.

FORD: After the seizure of Mrs Duncan by War Reserve Constable Cross, I did not order a search of every person in the room. The room was searched and the sheet was not found. I asked anyone who had the sheet to give it up.

LOSEBY: But did not a number of people clamour to be searched?

FORD: That is true.

LOSEBY: How do you account for the disappearance of the

sheet? It has been described many times how Mrs Duncan was searched before each sitting, her séance garments carefully examined and nothing white was ever found.

FORD: Someone in the audience must have had the sheet. Mrs Duncan was not searched because that would have required a doctor.

LOSEBY: She might have swallowed the sheet?

FORD: Yes.

LOSEBY: Is there anything, apart from swallowing, that might have required a doctor?

FORD: Yes. She might have secreted the sheet in another part of her body.

He was reluctant to specify which part and at this point the Recorder stated, "These are the merest speculations. You could say it was merely worthless speculation on his part and he would probably agree with you." The Recorder said that Loseby, if he wished, could state his views about where the sheet could have been concealed at another time.

LOSEBY: How many police were present?

FORD: There were eight policemen and detectives in the séance room and outside it.

LOSEBY: Yet no search was made of the people in the room?

FORD: That is correct.

LOSEBY: There was a policewoman present. She could have searched the women. Was it the police plan to take Mrs Duncan by surprise and catch her red-handed?

FORD: Yes.

The missing sheet was again the subject of questions when Cross was in the witness box and cross-examined by Loseby.

CROSS: I pushed aside the chair in front of me, seized Mrs Duncan by the arms and she was standing between the curtains hurriedly pushing a white cloth towards the floor. As I reached out to grasp her, the sheet dropped to the floor. Mrs Duncan stepped aside. I held her with my right arm and reached for the sheet with my left hand. I grasped it, but it began to move away. I still held her. I felt the cloth, which appeared to be a very flimsy substance; the nearest resemblance I can give is that it was like butter-muslin. I actually felt it and held it for a moment before it was pulled away. I stood up to pull away the curtains and the empty cabinet was clearly shown in the bright light of a torch. The sheet went towards the left, where the window was.

LOSEBY: It was clear, after this onslaught by you that Mrs Duncan was ill and was incapable of doing anything but groaning.

CROSS: I disagree with that.

LOSEBY: Did you like the task allotted to you?

CROSS: I was prepared to obey instructions.

He denied that he himself was ill that night, or that his hands were trembling after the seizure of Mrs Duncan, although counsel suggested it was plain to everyone in the room that something had happened to frighten him. He made his jump when the third figure had just appeared. He denied that he was grabbed by one of the sitters and that in falling forward through the curtain he fell on Mrs Duncan.

CROSS: I saw Mrs Duncan standing for approximately one minute at one side of the opening of the curtains.

LOSEBY: One minute is 60 seconds.

CROSS: It was approximately one minute. She was handed her shoes and she bent down to put them on.

LOSEBY: I suggest it was physically impossible for her to do so. The sheet must have passed three people. Yet none of these was searched, nor was Mrs Homer, though she was sitting near the window and in spite of the fact that she asked to be searched. I suggest that what happened was that you thought there might have been something, but when it slipped through your hands you knew that whatever else it was, it was not a sheet. Why, when there were several policemen present, was a search not made for a sheet?

CROSS: Nobody was interrogated who was sitting in the direction in which the sheet went.

Cross told the Recorder that he saw no difference in the forms which appeared.

Also on the second day of the hearing, Detective Taylor, said to be a photographic expert of the Portsmouth police, gave his opinion as to how he thought the spirit pictures shown to Fowler by Mrs Brown, had been produced. He had faked similar pictures.

LOSEBY: Do you have any experience of spirit pictures?

TAYLOR: No.

RECORDER: It comes to this, that you can fake a pictures as well as anybody else.

Charles Robert Burrell, a Portsmouth dockyard worker who described himself as a Spiritualist and a medium, said that at the first séance Albert had a nice masculine voice. Although the white material was called ectoplasm he did not think it was. Peggy, he said, was someone dressed up like a fairy in a Christmas pantomime and had a girlish voice. He told Loseby that he had attended only two materialisation séances in his life. He knew the Lock family, but denied they were disgruntled with Homers. He described himself as a semiskilled psychic investigator and had paid nothing for the two séances he had attended.

Loseby then explained the work of a materialisation medium, saying that for best results there should not be more than three sittings a week. If that was exceeded the medium might do herself an injustice.

LOSEBY: Are you telling the jury that spirits from another world manifest through you?

BURRELL: *I don't say that definitely.*

LOSEBY: *Do you conjure up spirits?*

BURRELL: *Never.*

LOSEBY: *Do you know any medium who could conjure up spirits?*

BURRELL: *No.*

LOSEBY: *Would you agree that it is the general attitude of mediums that they claim no merit or virtue of themselves, but seem to be used by outside forces?*

BURRELL: *Yes.*

LOSEBY: *You would agree that materialisation is a form of birth.*

BURRELL: *I can't follow you.*

LOSEBY: *If it were proved that when Mrs Duncan was entranced and ectoplasm was withdrawn suddenly, she was wounded, would that impress you?*

BURRELL: *That proves it.*

LOSEBY: *If that experiment had been carried out between the Portsmouth magisterial sitting and this, would it shake you?*

BURRELL: *Yes.*

Burrell said he was not "quite convinced" after the second séance, but "more convinced". Re-examined by Elam, he said he had read the works of Crookes. When he had gone to the séances he had expected to see something without darkness or without curtains. He saw no ectoplasm coming from Mrs Duncan. It was more like muslin or a sheet.

William Lock, a licensed pedlar from Portsmouth, told how one form came out of the side of the curtain, a distance of about eight feet, leaned over the row of seats in front of him and shook hands, with a hand "that was fat and clammy and more like a human hand than anything else."

LOSEBY: At the hearing at Portsmouth, in your evidence you stated, "It was very cold and flabby and a very fat hand."

LOCK: Yes. I did say that.

LOSEBY: Have you noticed that Mrs Duncan's hand is neither fat nor flabby?

Lock did not reply.

Mrs Emma K. E. Jennings, an ARP supervisor at Portsmouth, told the court that Peggy, who talked rapidly in a Scots accent, spoke to Christine Homer about some perfume taken from a bottle, about some lipstick she had tried but did not like and then asked Christine to kiss her. Christine did not do so. She had also heard Albert and was certain that his voice and that of Mrs Duncan were the same

LOSEBY: If, added to appearing like Peggy, Mrs Duncan spoke in various English dialects, that would be a difficult feat. It would be more difficult to explain how several different languages were also spoken. That would demand a rather cultured woman. You said previously that Peggy "sang and danced about in front of the curtain."

JENNINGS: She jigged about with a light movement and sang a little song. This was about 18 inches from the curtains.

LOSEBY: Did it occur to you that it would be a matter of difficulty for anyone impersonating to dance about outside the curtains?

JENNINGS: Yes. I had the feeling that it was not genuine.

LOSEBY: You have seen Mrs Duncan. Could it have been done by a woman as big as Mrs Duncan?

JENNINGS: The room was dark. It could have been.

Loseby then asked Mrs Duncan to stand up in the dock while he put the next question to Mrs Jennings. Mrs

Duncan did so.

LOSEBY: Do you think she could impersonate a slim young girl in such a way that she must have been plainly seen by some-body?

Mrs Jennings' reply was inaudible, if there was one.

Ernest H. Homer was the first witness for the defence. He told counsel that Mrs Duncan was paid £8 for each of the 13 séances she gave in January. The charge for each seat was 12s.6d. and there were 45 free seats at the whole series of sittings. Mrs Duncan was paid extra if the sitters exceeded 16 in number.

He described Albert's voice as "cultured Australian" and said it was nothing like Mrs Duncan's voice. Albert had invited Mrs Duncan to stand up and asked each sitter to see the outline of her face. Everyone had said they could see the outlines. Albert had opened the curtains. He was six feet tall and had a thin bearded face. Homer said he was nine inches or a foot away from the curtains. He saw Albert and the medium together and saw ectoplasm coming from the medium's mouth.

The first form had been that of an old lady who came out 3 ½ feet from the curtains. She had a thin, pointed face. Worth had said, "Are you an aunt of mine?" The figure had come to within six inches of his face and said, "Trying to act strange, aren't you?" Then it had disappeared. Albert had commented that it did not get much of a welcome. The height of the figure had been about 5 feet 2 inches.

Homer also told how a form, which was said to have been that of Worth's prematurely born sister, had appeared. Later, Worth had told Mrs Homer that he was so anxious to test the evidence that he had telephoned his mother and had confirmed that this was so.

Another figure had come for Mrs Homer and was that of

her grandmother. They had both joined in the singing of a Welsh hymn. The grandmother had been about 5 feet 3 inches tall, had a long face, an aquiline nose, grey hair parted in the centre and a mole on the right side of the nose.

The next form which appeared had been for Mrs Barnes. Homer had seen, between the parted curtains, a figure about 5 feet 10 inches tall, who said he would like to go back for his helmet. When he returned he had a white helmet, like a topi. The voice was a heavy, masculine one. Then had appeared the figure of a child about 3 feet tall. This figure spoke with a baby voice. She had gone up to Mrs Barnes, said to be her grandmother and taken her hand, saying as she played with her fingers, 'This little piggy went to market.'

Then had come the grab by Cross, who had said to Christine Homer when she had asked to be searched, "Be careful, or you will go down."

Cross-examined by prosecuting counsel John Maude, Homer said Mrs Duncan received about £112 for six days' work. The balance of £30-18s-9d. was given to several charities.

MAUDE: Have you heard about Mrs Duncan being examined and tested by the National Laboratory of Physical Science and coming away without the hall-mark of anything of the kind having happened?

Homer said he had seen the figure of Albert 20 times. Maude asked about the appearance of ectoplasm and said it was odd that no one seemed to see boots worn by the figures when they had seen a helmet worn by one. He also asked why Mrs Duncan wore black clothes and how the ectoplasm was connected to her.

MAUDE: Can you explain why the spirit forms could not be built up in front of you all?

HOMER: I believe they materialise in portions inside the cabinet.

MAUDE: Prefabricated! (There was laughter at this.) Can you also tell the court why Mr Taylor Ineson, who was at the séance, did not go into the cabinet at the invitation of his spirit brother?

HOMER: No.

MAUDE: Why would the spirit use the words 'bloody twisters'?

HOMER: These were not the words. What the spirit said was, "You were always bloody slow." It is important for people to speak as it encourages the spirits. Through Mrs Duncan's mediumship I have received evidence of my mother's survival.

Homer said that in the past two years The Master's Temple had given about £300 to charities. Homer also explained that the woman known as Mrs Homer was not his wife, at which the Recorder commented, "There maybe a perfectly good reason for it."

Wing-Commander Mackie began his evidence by saying, in reply to a question, that he would not call himself a Spiritualist, but he believed in Survival.

RECORDER: That is part of the Christian belief.

MACKIE: I was at a séance with Mrs Duncan on 3rd September, 1943 and the sitting of 19th January, was in the nature of a confirmation. On 3rd September, my mother materialised. We had an intimate conversation on things only we would know about. I was unknown to Mrs Duncan. My mother died in Australia in 1927. I leaned over until her face was about three feet away.

MAUDE: How did you recognise her?

MACKIE: A man knows his own mother. She was a slight woman of about seven to eight stone and had no marks on her face. Then my brother appeared and I said to him, "Gosh, Jack, have you still got your moustache?" It was close-cropped. Another figure was that of my sister Helen, who died before I was born.

MAUDE: Can you describe her?

MACKIE: It was a very lovely figure of a woman in a filmy robe. I could see the features of every form. I also saw a parrot materialise and knew every movement because I had a parrot at home. I knew the ridicule that would be poured upon me and that I would come in for some comment from the other officers.

Cross-examined, Mackie said he had decided to go to the séance on 19th January, at the last moment and when his mother appeared she remarked that she would not have materialised but for him. He knew his name was on the seat when he went into the séance, but he changed to another chair.

One by one, the witnesses gave evidence and were questioned. All quoted cases at Helen Duncan's séances where they had irrefutable proof that the materialised forms were those of their families and friends and could not in any way have been Helen Duncan impersonating them. They quoted conversations which could not have been known to Mrs Duncan.

William Colcher, a Portsmouth shopkeeper, present at the séance, was asked if a white sheet passed near him. He replied that if so he would certainly have seen it. He told Elam (prosecuting), that the "white milky substance" disappeared towards the cabinet - through the floor. All he heard Mrs Duncan talking about after she had been seized was her distressed condition.

Christine Homer, Mrs Homer's daughter, a nurse attendant, who was sitting at the end of the window seat, said Cross had pointed a finger at her and said, "It's you."

She had replied, "You have accused me wrongly," and had demanded to be searched. Cross refused and Miss Homer said she "got angry."

Marine Horace Llewellyn Clayton, another witness for

the defence was asked by the Recorder if it was the purpose of Spiritualism to try to contact departed spirits.

CLAYTON: *The purpose is to prove the after-life.*

RECORDER: *It is trying to establish the central fact of the Christian belief. It is not content to leave it where it is, but to prove it.*

Chapter 3

"Take then thy bond,
Take thou thy pound of flesh."

*****

Hannen Swaffer, the outstanding witness on the fifth day of the hearing, was introduced as "the well known journalist".

LOSEBY: You are also, I believe, a dramatic critic.

SWAFFER: I was, unfortunately.

LOSEBY: Unfortunately for whom?

SWAFFER: For me, my lord. I had to sit through it.

Swaffer said he had investigated psychic phenomena of every kind for 20 years, in many countries. He had investigated materialisation in this country and right across America.

LOSEBY: What was the purpose of these investigations?

SWAFFER: I believe it my duty to tell people the truth about the survival of their beloved dead.

Swaffer related accounts of his sittings with Helen Duncan. He had five or six sittings with her under test conditions, when there was a wide range of psychic phenomena. He explained how ectoplasm in materialisation exuded from mediums through the mucous membranes, the solar plexus and other parts of the body. It appeared to be a living substance. In Mrs Duncan's case the best likeness he could find for it was that it resembled living snow. He had seen ectoplasm about fifty times.

RECORDER: *When was the last time?*

SWAFFER: *Since this case was sent for trial.*

This was relevant because earlier in the day Loseby had asked that a test sitting, held in London on 15th March should be admitted as evidence. Swaffer and others attended this séance before the opening of the Old Bailey trial. There was some legal argument on the relevance of the evidence and finally the Recorder ruled that it could not be admitted, since it was under a cloud.

Loseby argued that the reason for holding a test séance was that he had proved Mrs Duncan was a genuine medium before the charge and he wanted to prove she was genuine after the charge.

LOSEBY: *Can you tell the court what part the sitters play in the production of physical phenomena?*

SWAFFER: *The more unity there is, the more blending there is of temperament, the easier it is for the phenomena to take place, just in the same way as you start conversation at a dinner party.*

LOSEBY: *Have you ever noticed any smell about ectoplasm at Mrs Duncan's séances?*

SWAFFER: *No, although I have been told about t. I have always sat with Mrs Duncan in a good red light, under which I could see right across the room. I have seen Mrs Duncan six or seven feet from the cabinet and the ectoplasm was coming from her nostrils.*

RECORDER: *In what year was this?*

SWAFFER: *After the case had been sent for trial. But I have seen the ectoplasm every time I have been to a séance with Mrs Duncan.*

LOSEBY: *Can you describe the ectoplasm a little more clearly. Could it be mistaken for butter-muslin?*

SWAFFER: Anybody who described ectoplasm as butter-muslin would be a child.

For days, counsel for the prosecution had dangled a piece of butter-muslin in court, asking witnesses whether ectoplasm looked anything like it.

SWAFFER: Under a red light, butter-muslin would turn yellow or pink. How could a red light make that kind of material take on a living whiteness?

RECORDER: What is it that causes ectoplasm to react to light?

SWAFFER: Just as the actinic properties of light affect and delay photographic processes, so does it affect ectoplasm. Under a red light ectoplasm appears white or a bluish white. The red light is not reflected in any way. In Mrs Duncan's case the ectoplasm is whiter than I have ever seen it. It is nonsense to say that the medium could conceal anything, as she was searched before entering the cabinet and could be seen in it.

Then Swaffer told how the sudden flashing of a light affected materialisation mediums. Once, he said, he took Mrs Duncan to a friend's house. All the people there were strangers to the medium. As there were some new sitters, he warned them carefully and deliberately that it would be dangerous to shine a light on the medium.

Unfortunately, Ernest Oaten, a well-known Spiritualist, had been speaking at the Queen's Hall and arrived late at the séance. He rapped on the door after it had started and Swaffer's accountant, a new sitter, who had arrived after the warning, lit his lighter, intending to help Oaten to enter the room. The séance had stopped and Helen Duncan bled profusely from the nose. She might have been seriously injured. Swaffer said he drew from the incident the conclusion that the medium was in a supernormal condition. In fact, one medium had been blinded for life in a similar way.

Loseby asked what other tests had been applied to Mrs Duncan. Swaffer described another test and was handed a document which he had signed on each page.

SWAFFER: *In 1932 I took with me four magicians - two professionals and two doctors who were amateurs. Mrs Duncan was tied up with 40 yards of sash cord. She was handcuffed with a pair of police regulation handcuffs. Her two thumbs were tied together so tightly that it cut into the flesh. All this was done by a professional magician, but the phenomena persisted. Although it had taken eight minutes for the magician to tie up the medium, she was freed from the cord, the thread and the handcuffs in three minutes. Houdini could not have done that.*

RECORDER: *Was Houdini one of the magicians?*

SWAFFER: *He was not.*

RECORDER: *How was she released?*

SWAFFER: *Her guide, Albert, released her, for no one else touched her.*

LOSEBY: *Do you know many actors?*

SWAFFER: *I know most of the actors on the London stage, although they might not admit they all know me.*

LOSEBY: *The point is to determine whether, in your opinion, Mrs Duncan and Albert were the same person, and whether a brilliant actor could simulate the parts.*

SWAFFER: *No. Albert has a distinct personality and a totally different approach to many things compared with Mrs Duncan. It is possible an actor could impersonate some things, but not a medium.*

ELAM: *(prosecuting) Could you describe Albert's voice in more detail?*

SWAFFER: *I have heard that it used to be Cockney and I have heard that it is an Australian voice. As a dramatic critic I find it difficult to describe voices.*

ELAM: Was it an Australian voice? Surely you have heard some.

SWAFFER: Yes, I heard Melba. It wasn't like her.

ELAM: So what kind of voice did Albert have? Was it an Oxford accent?

SWAFFER: There is no such thing as an Oxford accent. That is a BBC idea. It was a natural voice.

ELAM: When did you last hear it?

SWAFFER: Two weeks ago.

ELAM: Are you an expert?

SWAFFER: I have sat for 20 years. I have a home circle of my own.

ELAM: Are you a medium?

SWAFFER: No.

ELAM: Have you got a guide?

SWAFFER: My guide is an Egyptian.

ELAM: How do you know you have a guide?

SWAFFER: The guide of my home circle told me. He is an Indian.

The exchange had now become a contest between counsel and Swaffer, who insisted upon giving evidence in his own way. Answering a question on fraud, Swaffer said there had been accusations of fraud since the beginning of Spiritualism. "I have heard a lot about exposure. For 90 years we have had to stand that accusation. I have seen every possible test applied to Helen Duncan."

ELAM: You say 'every possible test'. Have electrical controls been applied? I understand the Austrian medium, Rudi Schneider, was brought to London for test séances by Mr Harry Price. Have you ever sat with him?

SWAFFER: I sat with Sir James Dunn and Lord Charles

Hope at Harry Price's laboratory, where a so-called electrical test was applied.

ELAM: This is the kind of test I refer to.

SWAFFER: That was not a real test and I myself had to point out how silly it was. Price's secretary, for instance, was walking about the room. I wanted a better test.

ELAM: Has Mrs Duncan been X-rayed, and has she ever taken a coloured pill?

SWAFFER: It has been done to her, swallowing blue pills which colour the contents of the stomach.

ELAM: What is the effect of prayer upon people seeking their dead in a room lit by a red light? Is the implication that it will make them more receptive?

SWAFFER: No. Sometimes this court opens with a prayer.

ELAM: Does prayer make people more receptive?

SWAFFER: Would prayer make people receptive to the sight of a bus? Besides, you must remember that many people are agnostics.

ELAM: When people attend a séance, is there any point in their sitting in the same place each time? Is a place assigned to them?

SWAFFER: It makes no difference at some séances, but at others, where the same people sit regularly, it helps, just as it helps if people take the same places at a dinner table.

Earlier in his evidence, Swaffer had held the piece of butter-muslin which was in court, in his hand. Loseby had asked him whether the phenomena he had seen at Mrs Duncan's séances could be explained by her swallowing that material. Swaffer replied that it would be impossible, as the material would become soggy and stained. Moreover, Mrs Duncan had a normal stomach. He held up a package of X-ray pictures of Helen Duncan's stomach, which showed it to be normal. He wished to show the photographs as evidence, but this was refused. Swaffer protested. Nor was he allowed to produce a doctor's certificate stating that the medium has a normal stomach.

SWAFFER: *I once tried to swallow some cheesecloth. May I try to swallow this?*

RECORDER: *No. I cannot reduce the court to the level of an exhibition.*

SWAFFER: *We can't be bothered with cheesecloth. Why have you got it here? We tried to get Harry Price to swallow it, but he would not. Never have I heard such nonsense - until Price invented this new lunacy of the cheesecloth. It is a silly invention of Price's.*

Elam returned to the incident of bleeding caused by someone entering a séance room and a light being flashed on. Had Swaffer examined the nose?

SWAFFER: *Yes. She has an ordinary nose. I saw blood coming from it.*

ELAM: *Did you look at it?*

SWAFFER: *What else does one do but look at a nose which is bleeding? Besides, I am a trained observer. My word is taken when I report other things.*

ELAM: *Are you a Spiritualist with fixed opinions?*

SWAFFER: *My opinions are fixed because they are based on evidence which is incontrovertible.*

ELAM: *When you were a dramatic critic, did other critics agree with your opinions?*

SWAFFER: *That is not a matter of fact, but a matter of opinion.*

ELAM: *I ask again, has Mrs Duncan been tested for the butter-muslin theory?*

SWAFFER: *I know that X-rays have been taken of her stomach. I have a medical certificate to say that she has an ordinary stomach.*

Witnesses continued through the day. They spoke of having attended Duncan séances, recognising relatives, seeing white ectoplasm, and hearing spirit forms speak in French, Dutch, Welsh, English and Arabic. There were also reports of Yorkshire and Lancashire dialects being spoken.

Reference was made during the evidence of Alfred Dodd, an author of works on the Shakespeare sonnets, to Mrs Duncan's previous conviction at Edinburgh in 1933. The jury was asked to leave while a legal discussion took place as to whether reference to the previous issue could be used. Loseby (defence) said he had talked with Maude (prosecution), and although there had been no agreement, he understood the previous conviction would not be raised. Because of that, he had refrained, according to the laws of evidence, all the way through the trial, from asking witnesses whether they thought Helen Duncan was genuine medium. Reference to a previous conviction could influence the jury's final verdict.

The Recorder said that as the defence had been allowed to go outside the actual events of the Portsmouth charges, there was some point in the prosecution plea to do the same. After referring to a legal precedent, he ruled that the Edinburgh prosecution could be mentioned before the jury. It would not be in order, however, to allow witnesses to describe test séances held after the prosecution was initiated in Portsmouth.

Upon the jury's return, Elam asked Dodd if he had heard of Mrs Duncan's previous prosecution in Edinburgh, when it was alleged that in pretending to be a medium she had dangled a woman's stockinette undervest to simulate a child.

Dodd said he had heard of the previous conviction, but he did not think it was the right verdict.

Loseby then asked the question he had hitherto refrained from asking, did the witness think that Helen Duncan was a genuine materialisation medium?

"She is a genuine materialisation medium," Dodd replied. "I am here because I owe her a debt. She is a genuine materialisation medium, and she is absolutely straight."

Throughout the questioning about the Edinburgh case, Helen Duncan was heard talking in a low voice in the dock. She broke down and cried when Dodds paid his tribute.

Dr John Winning, an assistant to the Medical Officer of Health of Glasgow, said he had sat with Mrs Duncan 40 times, and had seen 400 materialisations. He had heard many voices, several languages, and a number of dialects spoken by the materialisations at Mrs Duncan's séances. These included Scots, Irish, American, Hebrew and German. Once he had heard Gaelic spoken. It was impossible that Helen Duncan could have spoken those languages since she knew no language but her own.

From Edinburgh came J. W. Herries, chief reporter of 'The Scotsman'. He told of the spirit return of his friend, Sir Arthur Conan Doyle at a Helen Duncan séance, held in the home of an Edinburgh lawyer. Herries said he noticed the rounded features of Conan Doyle, saw his moustache, and observed the similarity of voice.

Herries was asked if he was a justice of the peace in Edinburgh. He explained that he was, but that in Scotland only a certain number of magistrates sat in court. The question was obviously leading to Mrs Duncan's previous conviction in the Edinburgh Sheriff Court. Herries said he knew of the trial, and had sat through it all in court. He did not agree with the verdict. He had been interested as a member of the committee of the Scottish Psychical Society, and Mrs Duncan had mistakenly given a sitting under the impression that it was for that society. Herries said the defence had been conducted by a young lawyer whose first case it was. It was a fact that the people who had brought the prosecution were among those who had benefited from the Duncan séance.

ELAM: You will recall that Mrs Duncan was caught trying to tuck a vest under her clothes when the light was put on.

HERRIES: Although I recall the case, I do not recall that.

LOSEBY: Could phenomena such as you witnessed have been faked by the use of an undervest?

HERRIES: That is ridiculous, and in line with the cheesecloth regurgitation theory, which is perfectly absurd.

Chapter 4

" There is no power in Venice
Can alter a decree established;
'T'will be recorded for a precedent,
And many an error, by the same example
Will rush into the state; it cannot be."

*****

Before the defence counsel's address to the jury, the Recorder asked them, "If you think any kind of demonstration is likely to assist you, I will consider the matter."

After a few moments the foreman of the jury said, "The general opinion is No."

This was the seventh day, and the Recorder, who had formerly rejected Loseby's offer of a demonstration without consulting the jury, had obviously changed his mind. Previously he had refused it as "a waste of time." Loseby began what was a two-hour speech for the defence. He said if it were proved that Helen Duncan was a cheat, a fraud and an impostor, then she was a person of no importance. "I want to say she is nothing of the kind," he said. "I say she is a person through whom a matter of vital importance to the world, more particularly at this time, had been proved. Through her mediumship hope has become a certainty."

His case was that Mrs Duncan had held herself to be a materialisation medium, a person through whom spirits from another world could make themselves visible. .

"The prosecution," said Loseby, "Instead of using plain,

simple, intelligible words of common law, under which all could have been charged with obtaining money under false pretences, went back to the Witchcraft Act of 1735 for the purpose of making Mrs Duncan look ridiculous - a kind of witch. Why this rigmarole of 200 years ago?

"The charge is that the four defendants conspired together at divers times to exercise a kind of conjuration. That involves a claim that Mrs Duncan can 'conjure up'. All she has claimed is that she is a medium, a term which explains itself. There is wide literature on the subject of materialisation, which includes contributions from Sir William Crookes, a president of the Royal Society."

There was no suggestion of conjuration of spirits in what Mrs Duncan or any genuine medium did, said Loseby. They said, in effect, that they were a kind of conduit pipe, through whom contact was made with the Other Side. The form of the séances was simple; there was a humble prayer to begin with, and then the Lord's Prayer.

"If there is conjuration in that, then every priest in the world would be guilty of conjuration. Every time a Roman Catholic priest ended his mass by praying for the communion of saints he would be exercising a kind of conjuration. But there has not been a word of evidence of conjuration. Is the Witchcraft Act of 1735 appropriate to this case at all?"

Dealing with the séances, Loseby said, "There is no fundamental difference in the acts of God exhibited in one way or another. God is showing Himself in another way, strange as it may seem, unacceptable as it may be, in humble surroundings in circumstances that the stupid might think ridiculous."

The real issue was whether the chief defendant was an impostor or not. An odious picture had been painted of the Portsmouth séances. Gill, one of the witnesses for the defence, said Loseby, had gone to one of Lord Dowding's meetings in Portsmouth, thinking Spiritualism was "a lot of hooey." But he was so impressed with what he heard that he went to see Mrs Duncan. As a result of what he saw there he was a hundred per cent convinced.

Explaining the evidence received by some of the witnesses, Loseby said it would be natural that Mrs Duncan, discovering she was a medium running considerable risks, even to the extent of endangering her life, should, as a canny Scot, decide to charge a fee for her sittings. Some of the sittings may not have been well managed. Mrs Brown may have said irrelevant things, and too many people may have been admitted to the séances.

The fees Helen Duncan charged were from £7 to £9 a sitting. If there was anything wrong in charging it would have been stated clearly in the indictment. There had been dreadful incompetence and folly by the Homers. They had held materialisation séances, with well over 20 people present, when some who had paid 12s.6d. would be unable to see properly, and therefore could presume fraud. But the Homers were not charged with that. Mrs Brown had been over-garrulous, and Mrs Homer had said foolish things.

Loseby examined in detail the evidence given by Worth, and said the defence did not admit that a single word said by him was true. Although the doctor had sat next to him at the séance, he said, the doctor did not corroborate a word which was said. With some care, the prosecution had not asked for that corroboration. That was important, because if the doctor's testimony went, only Worth was left as a witness for the prosecution.

Referring to evidence of different languages and dialects spoken by the materialisations, Loseby asked whether it was conceivable that Mrs Duncan was such a consummate actress that she could simulate all the characters, all the voices, all the languages and all the dialects manifested.

Examining the evidence of Spiritualists, who had come long distances, who were not stupid people, but who had shrewdly given their testimony in defence of their religion, he was interrupted.

The Recorder interposed, "This prosecution does not involve any attack on Spiritualism."

On the critical séance of 19th January, Loseby said the aim was to catch Mrs Duncan red-handed and to find the sheet. But it was abundantly clear that there was no sheet. It had never been found because it did not exist. The birth-marks, features, voices, the baby - they could not have been done by a sheet. He had offered Mrs Duncan to give a test séance at the beginning of the hearing, but that had been refused. In spite of that, he was sure the genuineness of Mrs Duncan's mediumship had been proved.

Maude, in the prosecution's address to the jury, paid tribute to the skill with which Loseby conducted the defence, and then derided some of the statements made by witnesses - the cat which miaowed, the rabbit and the parrot. He said that people who went to these séances saw what they wanted to see.

On the after-life as revealed by the séances, he said, "This is some other world. Where? - we don't know, with a setting we don't know, where people wear monotonous clothing, no shoes or boots - a dull sort of world."

Referring to the mutilated form which materialised at one séance, he asked, "How does it come about that Providence allows this monstrous shape to come? And why did not the cat come back, showing itself as it lay expiring when it was drowned?"

He described Albert, Mrs Duncan's guide as "a sort of commissionaire", and said, "Let me ask you to imagine an afternoon in the Other World. They are sitting round Mary

Queen of Scots. Her head is on. St. Sebastian, the pin - cushion saint, is there, perfectly normal. There are various persons who have been mutilated, looking perfectly all right. No arm or leg cut off, no eyes out. Then suddenly someone says something which is sad. Off comes the Queen's head - under her arm, I presume - St. Sebastian begins to bleed, and unmutilated persons become mutilated. It is absolutely fantastic. If this is the sort of thing we are coming to, it is time we began to pull ourselves together and exercise a little common sense."

On Loseby's indictment of the witnesses, Worth and Cross, Maude said, "Of the various criticisms of the people called by the prosecution, I do not intend to say a word."

Addressing the jury, he said, "Mr Hannen Swaffer will not pay the slightest attention to what you think."

He commented that it was curious that only the relatives of the credulous inquirers appeared, and obviously they saw only what they wanted to see. He asked why Jarvis's alleged phrase, "bloody twisters" had not been explained by putting his brother in the witness box. "It may be that we do not change when we pass on," he commented, "And Jarvis retains his robust language."

He contrasted the use of the word "bloody" with the prayers said at the opening of the séances, and asked why historical figures like Napoleon, Shelley, Keats, Socrates and Shakespeare did not return.

"As for the parrot which materialised," he added, "I use the Shelley reference: 'Hail to thee, blithe spirit, bird thou never wert.' For it was not a bird, but a fraud."

He brought in Browning's attack on 'Sludge, the Medium' and said that throughout the ages it had been recognised that dealing with occult powers was an opportunity for the fraudulent. Mrs Duncan, like all fraudulent mediums, picked up information because of the position she had gained as a kind of goddess. Worth's lie about telephoning his mother he said was a white lie to which he had to resort in order to catch the defendants.

He could see no conceivable reason why the curtains in a séance should be opened or closed, or why Mrs Duncan should have worn white or black clothing. He dismissed the languages spoken at her séances by saying that a smattering of languages would be easily learned by a person setting out to be fraudulent. There had been thousands of fraudulent mediums.

The Recorder's summing up, lasting nearly two hours, began with an explanation of The Witchcraft Act and the legal view of conspiracy.

"If Mrs Duncan, by going into a trance," he said, "Or simulating a trance, pretended to hold communion with the spirits, that was the kind of conjuration which is referred to in the Witchcraft Act. The emphasis is on the word 'pretend' and the offence, if there was an offence, began as soon as it was claimed to do that kind of thing.

"This case has exceeded all the bounds to which it should have been kept. Matters have been brought in beyond the Portsmouth séances - which is really what we were concerned with - and I have granted every indulgence. The prosecution, as framed, in no way attacks Spiritualism as a sect and it can not, by any possible exaggeration be magnified into anything but a charge of commonplace fraud. No religious persecution is involved."

Going through the evidence, he said the jury had to decide for themselves whether the witness Worth was to be believed, for his evidence was fatal to Mrs Duncan. On the matter of his changing his evidence, the jury might decide to disregard it on that account, but Worth had corrected his statement at the first opportunity. He pointed out that of the four defendants only Homer had gone into the witness-box. The defence had adopted a policy of not putting the other three defendants in the witness-box, and by that may have prevented them from saying something to their advantage.

The defence, he said, was entitled to the benefit of the fact that when the police made the search, nothing was found. The white sheet, or whatever it was, was said to be ectoplasm, but nobody had explained what ectoplasm was.

"Nobody," said the Recorder, "doubts that Spiritualism may have some value if a person has no belief in the Christian faith, or if their faith is so weak that they are unable to accept the Easter story of the Christian religion, in which the whole thing is summed up. Whether the general effect of Spiritualism is good or bad, who can say? I don't propose to make any comments."

"All that the witness Mr Hannen Swaffer had to say was to contradict some of the others, not altogether to be wondered at."

He quoted witness Abdy Collins, who thought there might be an emotional tendency at séances. "The jury might think that accounts for a great deal."

Of the offer of a test sitting, he said that if Albert did not come to Mrs Duncan's aid it might operate unfairly against her. He did not think it was something with which the jury should be associated.

After twenty-five minutes the jury returned. The four defendants had been found guilty of conspiracy to contravene the Witchcraft Act. The jury was told by the clerk that they were discharged from giving verdicts on any of the other counts.

Chief Constable A. C. West of Portsmouth said that Mrs Duncan was born in Callander, Perthshire, educated at school there, and was married to a cabinet maker. They had a family of six, with ages ranging from 18 to 26, and now lived in Edinburgh. Mrs Duncan had been a so-called Spiritualist for many years, and was well known in Edinburgh as such. She spent much of her time travelling the country as a medium. So far as he could discover, neither she nor her husband paid income tax.

In 1933, said West, she was convicted in Edinburgh. He began to read an extract from the Procurator Fiscal at Edinburgh relating to that case, in the course of which it was stated that when challenged by a woman at a séance, Mrs Duncan said, "I'll brain you", and swung a chair, striking two people in the audience.

At this point Mrs Duncan said from the dock, "I never did."

"She has been coming to Portsmouth for the past five years," said West. "Apart from the fact that she has not been in trouble since 1933, I can find no redeeming feature in her character. Not only has she attempted to delude the confirmed believers in Spiritualism, but she has tricked, defrauded and preyed on the minds of a certain credulous section of the public who have gone to these meetings in search of comfort of mind in their sorrow and grief, and many of whom left with the firm conviction that the memory of the dead had been besmirched. She thought fit to come to Portsmouth, the first naval port of the world, where she will find bereaved families."

Here the Recorder commented, "She may have been invited." "In 1942," West went on, "Mrs Duncan was reported for having transgressed the security laws when she foretold the loss of one of His Majesty's ships before the fact was made public. She is an unmitigated humbug and pest."

West said of Homer that he came from Staffordshire. He had no previous convictions and had a good character. He was a dispenser and not a qualified chemist. The police had known people who had convictions practising as mediums at the temple above Homer's house.

Mrs Homer, who was 50, came from Newbridge, Monmouthshire, and had been separated from her husband, George Arthur Jones, for 24 years. She married at the age of 19 and during the First World War had travelled in France with theatrical companies, entertaining the troops. She had been connected with the Spiritualist movement for 15 years, and in 1940 the room at Copnor Road was registered as a Spiritualist Church. The police had traced receipts which showed that the church had handed some £450 to charities.

Mrs Brown, who came from County Durham, was married to a colliery mechanic in 1913. In 1929 she was convicted of larceny at Marlborough Street. A month later she was sentenced in Sunderland for shoplifting. Mrs Brown, said West, encouraged people to attend performances and acted as "prompter" to the audience.

The Recorder announced that he would pass sentence on Monday, three days later. As Mrs Duncan was led weeping from the dock, she said in a broad Scots accent, "I never heard so many lies in all ma life. I dinna ken they should get away with thae lies."

Before passing sentence on Monday morning the Recorder named the four defendants and said, "You have been found guilty of conspiring together to commit an unlawful act, namely, of pretending to recall spirits of deceased persons in visible and tangible form; the emphasis, of course is on the word 'pretending'. Whether genuine manifestations of the kind are possible, the verdict does not decide, and this court has nothing whatever to do with any such abstract questions.

"The jury found that the method adopted by you in the

exhibitions covered by the charge amounted to fraud upon those who witnessed them. It has been argued that the statute of 1735, which makes such pretending an offence, is old and out of date. But fraud existed long before that statute was passed, and has prevailed in one form or another ever since. It has also been suggested that Mrs Duncan should be allowed to give a demonstration of her powers. As I have already said, if this had taken place and nothing had appeared, Mrs Duncan would have been condemned even before she had been tried. It would have been in effect a reversion to the Dark Ages and to something very akin to trial by ordeal.

"It was not a question of Mrs Duncan taking a risk, but a question of her being tried according to the laws of the land. There is nothing in this prosecution directed against Spiritualism as such, and all those who may believe in genuine manifestations of a spiritual kind will, I imagine, welcome the expulsion of fraud.

"In law there is no uncertainty at all about the position of Spiritualists, among whom there are many sincere and devoted persons. They are free to go their own way, and they are only responsible to the law when fraudulent practices are proved. In this respect they are no different from any other section of the community. In this case the jury appeared to have little hesitation in finding that all of you have participated in a common fraud, and I just deal with the case upon that finding.

"There are many people, especially in wartime, searching for their loved ones. There is a great danger of their susceptibilities being exploited, and out of this yearning for comfort and assurance there are those, unfortunately, who are ready to profit.

"Many of these persons who seek this solace are trusting by nature, and in poor circumstances. The law endeavours to protect such persons against themselves. In this case Mrs Duncan made £112 in six days, which is some indication of how willing people are to dabble in the occult. That being so, it is highly important, in the interests of the community as a whole, that these demonstrations should be conducted without fraud.

"I have considered very anxiously the course I should take and I have come to the conclusion that, as the jury have found, this a case of plain dishonesty, I can make no distinction between the accused. In the case of Mrs Duncan it is she who has made the most out of this, and the sentence I impose upon her is nine months."

Helen Duncan, standing in the dock, shouted, "I didn't do anything!" She seemed to swoon and was heard moaning. After a few seconds she recovered and repeated that she had not done anything. "Oh, God! Is there a God?" she cried out.

Addressing Mrs Brown the Recorder said, "It is a long time ago since you were convicted for shoplifting. I dismiss this from my mind altogether. You took an active part, particularly by the exhibition of these photographs. It is quite true they are so crude that one would hardly imagine they would deceive anybody. But you were trying to impress upon people the genuineness of this exhibition by the handling of these photographs. The matter, therefore, cannot be passed over in this case. The sentence of the court upon you is one of four months' imprisonment."

To Ernest Homer and Elizabeth Jones (Homer) he said, "You are in a different position. It might well be that your enthusiasm led you to close your eyes to what was going on.

"You have good characters, and I do not think it necessary to pass sentence of imprisonment on either of you. I trust that in future you will be on your guard against those who are only too ready to make money at the expense of credulous people. I intend, therefore, to give you the benefit of the doubt, and bind you over to be of good behaviour for two years in your own recognisance of five pounds."

Loseby then asked the Recorder for a certificate of appeal, saying that there were three difficult matters in this case. The first was whether the Witchcraft Act applied to this case at all. The second was the offer of the test of Mrs Duncan's powers, made in his opening speech. He submitted that it would have been in the nature of a medical examination, and might have been conclusive in favour of Mrs Duncan. But it might also have been totally wrong.

"It would be unfortunate if, say, three months elapsed until the appeal was decided, and Mrs Duncan was kept in prison. It might thereafter be decided that the trial should be quashed. It would help me in the appeal if the whole matter was sub judice."

"I do not see that this case deserves a certificate," replied the Recorder.

Referring to the Press, Loseby said some newspapers had been rather free with their headlines throughout the trial. The matter would be *sub judice* within two hours, and that knowledge might assist the Press.

"I would say that you have been rather tempting to the Press," said the Recorder.

Chapter 5

".. Earthly power doth then show likest God's
When mercy seasons justice."

*****

Although Sir Gerald Dodson refused to grant Loseby a certificate of appeal, the Lord Chief Justice and two other judges of the Court of Criminal Appeal could not, after a two day hearing, give their judgement. They announced that it would have to wait for the next sitting.

It was on 3rd April, 1944 when Mrs Frances Brown was sentenced to four months' imprisonment. The Appeal Court did not deal with her case until 8th June, when, because of remission, she was due to leave Holloway Prison. But because of the pending result of the Appeal, her remission was suspended. Judgement was not given until 19th June.

The defence lawyers had to make application "for leave to appeal", and this application became the Appeal, which was against the conviction of the four defendants. Mrs Duncan appealed against her sentence of nine months, but Mrs Brown did not appeal against her four month sentence.

The grounds for appeal were:

1. The indictment as drawn discloses no offence under the Witchcraft Act, 1735, and should be quashed.

2. Sir Gerald Dodson, Recorder of the Old Bailey, wrongly directed the jury that a pretence to hold communion with spirits of deceased persons constituted an offence

under the Witchcraft Act, 1735.

3. There is no evidence of any acts by the accused which constituted an offence under the Witchcraft Act, 1735.

4. The Recorder wrongly rejected evidence of an examination by Helen Duncan, purporting to demonstrate and prove that at all material times she was a materialisation medium and to disprove the allegations against her.

5. The Recorder failed to direct the jury on the law of the case, or as to the facts of the case, and in particular on the following matters: -

(a) He failed to review the evidence or adequately to review the evidence as to the conspiracy alleged.

(b) He failed to sum up the evidence given for the defence, or to review it with reasonable accuracy, or in any way to explain or do reasonable justice to the evidence given for the defence.

(c) He wrongly asserted to the jury and without any foundation in fact, that "for reasons best known to themselves the defence had thought it necessary to fortify the case by using the resources of the community of Spiritualists."

(d) He wrongly allowed evidence of a previous conviction.

6. The Recorder exhibited bias throughout.

7. There was no evidence sufficient to found the conviction.

8. The verdict of the jury was against the weight of the evidence. The verdict of the jury was unreasonable and perverse.

9. The trial was unsatisfactory, and there was a miscarriage of justice.

The three judges who heard the appeal were the Lord Chief Justice (Viscount Caldecote), Mr Justice Oliver and Mr Justice Birkett.

During the two days in which the appeal was argued, it became obvious that the fate of Helen Duncan hung on the interpretation which would be given to the word "conjuration". All the arguments centred on this word.

Loseby's case was that the Witchcraft Act could not possibly apply in this instance. He had spent weeks referring to legal textbooks, defining the question of "conjuration".

For two days the Appeal Court argued over a pile of books, some going back to the time of Henry VIII, Queen Elizabeth, James I and George II. There were even arguments about the Old and New Testament, and about the Woman of Endor, wrongly described as the Witch of Endor. Dictionaries were consulted, one after another, as to the precise meaning of "conjuration". Throughout the two days the Appeal Court was packed with people who had come to listen.

There was discussion over one of the grounds for appeal - that the Recorder had exhibited bias:

CALDECOTE: Mr Loseby, do you infer that the Recorder had a crooked motive, a twist, that he was improperly biased?

LOSEBY: No, my lord.

CALDECOTE: Do you withdraw that complaint?

LOSEBY: The learned Recorder seemed unable to get from his mind a certain distaste for the whole subject. Not a question was put by him, from beginning to end, to assist me.

BIRKETT: Assuming the judge takes the view that human credulity could go no further, surely that is not bias? Must he be mealy-mouthed?

LOSEBY: It is not an unknown thing for a learned judge to exhibit bias. I withdraw the suggestion that the bias was an improper one, but the learned Recorder had preconceived ideas on the subject of Spiritualism.

BIRKETT: Had the Recorder been in your favour, would the defence have complained?

LOSEBY: I would not have been appearing in front of you, my lord, had that been the case.

OLIVER: Regarding the complaint that the jury were misdirected, and wherein you say bias was apparent, the judge did state that there was no attack on Spiritualism.

LOSEBY: If I may say so, my lord, that only made it worse. What was said was, 'Nobody doubts that Spiritualism may have some value if a person has no belief in the Christian faith, or if that faith is so weak that they are unable to accept the Easter story of the Christian religion in which the whole thing is summed up. Whether the general effect of Spiritualism is good or bad, who can say?' It is plain that this implies that Spiritualism is of no value, that it is anti-Christian, or at any rate, of no value to a Christian person. Comments were also made on the witnesses for the defence. In my view, the essence of their testimony was omitted from the summing-up. My defence was never put by the learned Recorder. It is apparent to me, that after the direction in the summing up,

Mrs Duncan's conviction was almost certain. The learned Recorder totally and completely failed to do justice to the evidence for the defence. Indeed, he did not do justice to one witness for the defence. The conviction was against the sheer weight of the evidence.

OLIVER: You have no right to say the jury did not examine the evidence.

LOSEBY: That is what I do say. My offer of a demonstration, which I regarded as the acid test of Mrs Duncan's powers, was refused. This demonstration would have been short, easy, and practicable. How can this test in justice be refused?

BIRKETT: Could the jury have handled the parrot and rabbit when they materialised?

Loseby made a plea for the defence of all new learning and knowledge, pointing out that every advance in human understanding had always been received with incredulity and scepticism.

"I cannot understand why the Recorder disallowed the witnesses who were going to describe test séances held a few days before the Old Bailey proceedings. These were in the nature of a medical examination. They would have given a certificate which would have vouched for the fact that Mrs Duncan's mediumship was still functioning.

"It was also said in the summing-up that some of the things the jury had heard described by witnesses might have been due to ecstasy, whereas all the witnesses were reliable and sober-minded people. Indeed, one of them had seen over a thousand materialised forms. The Recorder did not point out the importance of evidence of that kind. Nor did he refer to the contradiction in the police evidence over Mrs Duncan being seen standing up when the light was flashed on. All the evidence for the defence was that she was sitting down.

"I would also remind the court that one of the persons selected to test Mrs Duncan a few days before the trial was a Church of England clergyman, the Rev. Maurice Elliott, whose evidence was disregarded at the Old Bailey.

"I realised when I first took over the defence that a difficult task was before me. I decided, rightly or wrongly, that the one way to establish the defendant's innocence was to give evidence of her materialisation mediumship during the past, at the Portsmouth séances, which were the subject of the prosecution, and at sittings held after the time the police had intervened."

Maude, who had appeared for the prosecution at the Old Bailey, addressed the judges and contended that according to Section 3 of the Witchcraft Act there could be no prosecution for communing with spirits. He rebutted Loseby's contention that the offence was for "conjuring up evil and wicked spirits." In his view, the words "any kind of witchcraft, sorcery, enchantment or conjuration" took in every form of conjuration, whether good or evil spirits were involved.

This provoked another consultation of books, in an effort to establish not only the meaning of "conjuration" but of the word "pretend".

The points of the appeal were individually examined, Loseby explaining how he proposed at the Old Bailey to introduce the test of Helen Duncan's mediumship. Had he been permitted, he would have put her in the witness-box and asked how her powers worked. He would then have asked her if she was willing to undergo a test, and then it would have been for the Recorder, and later the jury to decide whether a test was wanted. Loseby maintained that by asking the witness if she could produce there and then, it would have been no surprise and no embarrassment to the court. It would have been dignified and fair. If a test had been held, he would have asked for the production of a voice in full light, and then for the voice in a good red light. He would have tried to reproduce, as far as possible, conditions of the Portsmouth séances.

When the Lord Chief Justice pointed out that Loseby did not call his client at all, the reply was that he could not for ordinary purposes, as everything happened at her séances while she was in trance. He quoted the case of Rex. v. Lawrence in 1877, when counsel in this case concerning a medium was asked why he did not ask his client to give a demonstration to prove his powers.

The Lord Chief Justice said that the Recorder had decided to follow the ordinary procedure. Loseby responded by saying that, guided by the case he had quoted, he had tried on three different occasions when he thought it appropriate, to offer the test. The Recorder had made it clear that if he had called Mrs Duncan when he had wanted to, he would not allow certain questions to be put to her. Loseby added that he was in difficulty because the Recorder had asked him to decide immediately what to do. Since he was not going to be allowed to give the evidence he wished to give, he decided not to call Mrs Duncan at all.

He said he believed Mrs Duncan had every right to the test, and had she been allowed to give it, it would have ensured her acquittal. "It was not for the jury to say whether they wanted a test," he stated, "Because they could not give a right verdict unless they did have one. First the honourable Recorder refused it, and then at a later stage asked the jury whether they wanted it. And I regarded it as an acid test."

Loseby quoted some of the oldest English legal authorities, Coke and Blackstone, to support his contention that the charge should not have been brought under the Witchcraft Act. He examined all Acts leading up to the Witchcraft Act to show that because of the beliefs of those days nothing else was meant except the prosecution of people for "traffic with evil spirits."

His other contention was that it was only an offence under the Witchcraft Act to pretend to conjure up evil spirits, and that to do so in reality would be no offence at all – for the Act did not recognise their existence.

Then came discussion on the difference between conjuration and witchcraft. It was held that, by the old statutes, conjuration meant using the name of God to summon the Devil, and then compelling him to do your will, whereas witchcraft implied a previous compact with the Devil, under which he did things in return for a terrible price. It was made clear that a witch made chants.

Quoting from ancient dictionaries, Loseby recited some of the definitions, showing that they merely reflected the beliefs of the time. But, he pointed out, this was 1944 and nobody now believed in witchcraft. Yet the seriousness of the situation was that the Witchcraft Act was the lineal descendant of Acts of Parliament in which punishment for witchcraft was burning!

While these points were being argued in the Appeal Court, the prisoners sat some distance away, Helen Duncan sometimes weeping and Mrs Brown, unmoved for the most part, occasionally broke down.

Hawkin, another legal authority, was quoted, and Loseby said that the essence of the whole case was plainly set out in Dalton's 'County Justice' of 1727. There it was stated, before the passage of the Witchcraft Act, that the offence was always "trafficking with a familiar spirit." Witches had familiar spirits, but it was all ancient superstition and could give no support to this prosecution, which should never have been brought under the Witchcraft Act.

Examining the evidence for the existence of the alleged white sheet which had "disappeared", Loseby said there was indeed something white, but it was ectoplasm.

"The honourable Recorder did not point out sufficiently that nothing was found - neither the sheet nor apparatus," said Loseby. "Nor did he explain the difficulty of the Crown case. How could Mrs Duncan simulate a child? How could she speak in foreign languages and dialects, and how did she obtain the likenesses which caused people to recognise their relatives and friends?"

On the question of bias, Loseby said many comments had been made by the Lord Chief Justice on Spiritualism, but the honourable Recorder had made a comment, which he objected to, stating that the defence was using all the resources of the Spiritualist community to show that Mrs

Duncan was a genuine medium. "It is being said, in effect," he said, "That the case was propped up, and that witnesses did not come forward solely in the interests of truth."

After a few minutes whispered consultation, the Lord Chief Justice announced that judgement would be given at the next sitting of the Criminal Court of Appeal on 19th June.

Chapter 6

"Nothing but the plenty."

*****

The judgement of the Appeal Court was given in the inauspicious surroundings of an air raid shelter! A flying bomb had hit the Law Courts, and about fifty people crowded together on wooden benches. Reporters and KC.s sat cheek by jowl with defendants and members of the public. Because of the rapidity with which Lord Caldecote read the judgement, it was difficult for reporters to take it all down accurately. Maurice Barbanell, a few days later, sent a representative to the office of the Criminal Court of Appeal, to ask for a copy. He quotes the following incident:-

"When he courteously made his request, he was sternly questioned as to who he was. He explained that he had come from 'Psychic News'.

'What's that?' he was asked.

'A Spiritualist newspaper,' came the reply.

'Who sent you?' was the next question.

'The Editor.'

Thereupon the official made the extraordinary outburst, 'You can tell him to go to hell!'

Having delivered this needlessly abusive ejaculation, the official then said that a copy of the judgement could be obtained only through a solicitor."

Barbanell recounted all these facts in a letter of complaint he sent to the Lord Chief Justice, saying the judgement was of vital importance to the whole Spiritualist movement. Surely they were entitled to known about a legal decision which might turn a million people into criminals. Spiritualists, like other citizens, paid the salaries of all judges and law officials. There was no excuse for downright rudeness.

"I received a reply from Caldecote," says Barbanell. "He expressed his regret for any discourtesy on the part of an official of the Criminal Appeal Court Office. He made full enquiries, he said, but nobody in that office could now remember exactly what had happened. 'You will realise that tempers are frayed at the present time,' Lord Caldecote's letter ended, 'and this may be the explanation of any unintentional discourtesy.'"

Every ground of the appeal was dismissed. The Recorder was upheld in all he had said and done at the Old Bailey trial. The main points of the appeal judgement were at follows:

"The indictment contained seven counts, the first of which was of conspiracy to contravene the provisions of Section 4 of the Witchcraft Act, 1735.

"In the particulars of offence it was alleged that these four appellants 'conspired together, and with other persons unknown, to pretend to exercise or use a kind of conjuration, to wit, that through the agency of the said Helen Duncan, spirits of deceased persons should appear to be present, in fact in such place as the said Helen Duncan was then in, and that the said spirits were communicating with living persons then and there present.'

"The trial had then proceeded on Count 1 of the indictment only.

"The case for the prosecution was that the whole performance was an elaborate pretence, a fraudulent performance, a mere imposition on human credulity.

"There was evidence for the jury which, if believed, would be evidence of a pretence that so-called materialisations, which were in fact produced by means of fraudulent devices and apparatus, were of a different nature altogether.

"The witnesses for the defence, who were present on the material dates, gave evidence denying that there were any elements of pretence or deception.

"The jury had before them, in great fullness, the evidence on both sides as to the facts, and had before them with equal fullness the submissions of counsel upon these facts.

"In addition to the witnesses called for the defence, who were present at the sittings which were the subject of the indictment, the defence called no less than 26 witnesses who were not present, but who gave evidence about Mrs. Duncan's performances as a medium over a long period of years, expressing their genuineness and informing the jury of the mysteries of the spirit world, the nature of ectoplasm and a variety of matters of that kind.

"We find it a little difficult to see on what principle that evidence was admitted in this case. The relevant period was the period covered by the indictment. The relevant enquiry was whether the appellants had conspired, as alleged on these dates, to pass off a sham on their audience, and whether the appellant Duncan had taken part in the alleged conspiracy.

"To examine what took place on other occasions scarcely seems relevant to the charge. The learned Recorder no doubt was anxious that in an unusual case some latitude should be given, and permitted the evidence to be called.

244

But had he excluded it, we do not think complaint could properly have been made. Indeed, we think it would have been rightly excluded.

"In the course of the eight days of the trial at the Central Criminal Court, all the evidence given by witnesses, who were subjected to detailed cross-examinations, and explained at considerable length by counsel, was before the jury. The jury convicted the appellants on Count 1 in the indictment, the only count on which the trial had proceeded.

"Ground 4 is a complaint that the learned Recorder wrongly rejected evidence by the appellant Duncan purporting to demonstrate and prove that at all material times she was a materialisation medium and to disprove the allegations against her.

"In the course of the argument in this court, the learned counsel for the appellants conceded that it was a matter for the discretion of the learned Recorder whether to allow such a demonstration to be given or not.

"The difficulty of arranging such a demonstration, satisfactory in all its detail to both sides, is obvious. To mention only one matter: if in the course of the demonstration, ectoplasm was to be alleged to emanate from the medium, would the jury be allowed to handle it, or to do anything to verify the appearance? Or would the jury have to be content with what they could see in a dim light, such as was provided on the occasions in question?

"A host of similar difficulties can be seen both from the point of view of the prosecution and of the defence.

"It seems clear to us that no such demonstration, even if the circumstances in which it should take place could be agreed and whatever it purported to show, could be conclusive on the only issue which the jury had to try, and indeed might well confuse the jury, or operate to the great disadvantage of the appellants.

"We think the learned Recorder exercised his discretion wisely in this case, and we may add that he was fortified in what he did by the answer of the jury to the question he asked them as to whether they wished to see such a demonstration. No reasonable ground of complaint can be sustained on this point.

"The next ground is in reality the same ground of complaint as appears in Ground 4, though expressed in a different form. It is that the learned Recorder wrongly rejected evidence of an examination by expert witnesses on 15th March, 1944, to prove that the appellant Duncan was a genuine materialisation medium.

"We think this evidence was rightly excluded as being irrelevant to the issue before the jury. An examination, by expert witnesses in March 1944, could not assist to determine the truth of the facts alleged to exist upon another date.

"Ground 6 is a complaint of the learned Recorder's direction to the jury on the law and on the facts. The main complaint is that the defence was not adequately placed before the jury.

"At every stage of the eight day trial, the main issue or indeed the only issue of fact in the case was before the jury in almost every word that was said, either by the witnesses or by counsel. The prosecution alleges that it was all a sham, the defence asserted with a wealth of witnesses that everything was completely genuine.

"The learned Recorder could not be expected to repeat the evidence of eight days, but he did review before the jury the main points of the evidence, and told the jury what the question was that they had to decide. We think he succeeded, within reasonable limits of time, in reminding the jury of the evidence that had been given for the defence.

"It would be unreasonable to expect the learned Recorder to comment on each piece of evidence, and indeed it was not necessary when the essential matter to which all evidence was directed, was so plainly before the jury from the first moment to the last.

"For a criticism of this kind to succeed, the appellant must show that the misdirection of the presiding judge was such, and the circumstances of the case were such, that it is reasonably probable that the jury would not have returned their verdict had there been no misdirection, and the burden of establishing this is upon the appellant. It is really impossible to say there was any such misdirection here.

"The case for the appellant had been laid before the jury with great fullness by the learned counsel for the defence, and the details of the evidence most forcibly presented, and it was not necessary that it should all be rehearsed again by the learned Recorder.

"A further ground of appeal was taken before us that the learned Recorder wrongly admitted evidence of a previous conviction of the appellant Duncan. Twenty-six witnesses at least were called especially to prove that the appellant Duncan was a materialisation medium of standing and repute.

"The evidence was most plainly admissible and proper in order that the jury might be informed not only of part of the facts, but of the whole of them.

"Further grounds of appeal were that there was no evidence to found the conviction, that the verdict of the jury was against the weight of evidence, that the verdict of the jury was unreasonable and perverse, and that the trial was unsatisfactory and there was a miscarriage of justice.

"We cannot find anything of substance in any of these

contentions.

"The trial was certainly unusual in its form, but if there was anything unsatisfactory about it, it was rather in the great latitude accorded to the defence in the conduct of the case, and the reception of evidence which, in a strict view of the law of evidence, should have been excluded."

The appeal result then went on to dissect the meanings of vital wording, and the historic legal aspects of the various Acts pertaining to the case. The final paragraph was as follows:

"We think these appeals against conviction should be dismissed. The application of the appellant Duncan for leave to appeal against this sentence should also be dismissed. On the footing of the verdict of the jury, nine months' imprisonment was, in our opinion, in no way excessive."

The judgement stated that the Appeal Court had decided - though it need not have done so - that the sentences should run from the date of conviction. Mrs. Brown, said Lord Caldecote, would be released that day. Helen Duncan returned to Holloway to complete her sentence.

This was not the end of the matter, and the defence applied to have the case of Helen Duncan brought to the House of Lords, the supreme judicial authority. This meant that a fiat had to be granted by the Attorney-General. He refused to grant this, on the grounds that the case was not a matter of public importance. Legally then, this was the end of the road, and nothing more could be done.

Chapter 7

"You take my life,
When you do take the means
whereby I live."

*****

The result of the Helen Duncan case provoked comment in many journals. Not unnaturally, one of the first Fleet Street men to leap into print was Hannen Swaffer, who had been a prominent witness for the defence. In 'The Leader' he wrote: -

"If the Witchcraft Act had been invoked at the time, it would have made Sir William Crookes a criminal because he sat with Florence Cook (a famous materialisation medium), Queen Victoria a criminal because she sat with John Brown, Sir Oliver Lodge a criminal because he sat with Mrs. Osborne Leonard, and Lord Dowding a criminal because he sat with Estelle Roberts. I, according to the decision, have been a criminal hundreds of times.

"Dowding, who led the Battle of Britain, is now going round the country telling vast audiences how dead airmen have returned to him with messages of comfort for their families. He has dried many tears. Yet for making himself able to do this by attending séances, he is apparently as guilty as the Portsmouth people who were convicted of 'conspiring' with Helen Duncan. Why was the Witchcraft Act dug up by the Crown in the year 1944? Surely, somewhere, a Hidden Hand is at work."

The 'Police Review' unexpectedly commented:-

"How, then, do genuine psychical researchers stand as a result of it? Most intelligent and careful people reserve a corner of their minds for the possibility that some so-called psychic phenomena may be within the reach of genuine experience.

"It seems to us that they may well regard the case with some disquiet. As it stands, since the charges alleging fraud and public mischief were not the subject of any verdict, it may well mean that all meetings of spiritualists are unlawful conspiracies, on the ground that they all involve 'a pretence to exercise conjuration' - i.e. a representation (not necessarily false) that the spirits of people who have died can be called up and conversed with.

"If this be so, the spiritualists may still feel uncon-vinced by the Home Secretary's assurance of last November that prosecutions will be confined to cases of fraud and imposture, so that 'persons bona fide engaged in the ministrations of the spiritualist churches' and in psychical research should not find themselves hampered by the provisions of the Law."

'The Solicitor' commented:-

"The present situation, in which both spiritualists and quacks are prosecuted under two obsolete Acts, is highly unsatisfactory, and calls for investigation."

Before the case of Helen Duncan came to court there had been three previous prosecutions this century under the Witchcraft Act - in 1904, 1935 and 1939. The two latter cases were for fortune-telling. Using the Duncan case as a precedent, the police charged another woman with the offence of pretended conjuration, a few months later. She was aged 72, and a cripple, and no doubt these two factors accounted for her being bound over when the case went to the Old Bailey.

A meeting due to be held on Sunday, 8th October, 1944 (four months after the Duncan case), at Stamford Hall, Altrincham, near Manchester, was banned by the police. It was to be a trance address by Dr Letari, spirit guide of W. H. Lilley, the famous healer. He was billed to speak through his medium on 'The Science of Spiritual Healing'. The police stated that the proceedings would be illegal because they amounted to conjuration.

Seven days after Helen Duncan's release from Holloway, the Freedom Fund committee of the Spiritualists' National Union issued the following statement: -

> "We have been entrusted with the task of doing everything possible to secure justice for mediums, and seek the aid of all persons interested in justice, and the honour of British justice.

> "Helen Duncan, in the month of March 1944, was charged under the Witchcraft Act, 1735, at the Central Criminal Court, and upon 3rd April 1944, was convicted and sentenced to nine months' imprisonment.

> "We are satisfied that Helen Duncan, like those charged with her, was completely innocent of the charge of pretending brought against her, that her trial violated elementary principles of justice, and that she was wrongly convicted.

> "In the course of the trial Helen Duncan wished to give evidence which she believed and which we believe, to be final and conclusive, that she had not pretended to be a medium, but that she was a medium. She wished, further, to tender the evidence of experienced and expert persons to the same effect, but was not allowed

to do so.

"Helen Duncan was charged under an Act which is antiquated and obsolete. In the course of the case, rules relating to procedure and evidence were laid down which, in our view, render inevitable the conviction of any innocent person similarly placed.

"Helen Duncan was released from Holloway Prison on Friday, 22nd September, and announced that she was not willing to offer her services as a medium again to any person, whether purporting to act for scientific or religious purposes, or any other purpose.

"Materialisation mediums of the kind and type of Helen Duncan are rare. Her decision constitutes a grave blow to investigation, advance and progress. For the reasons given above, we were unable to advise Helen Duncan to offer her services again. We are satisfied that she would be exposed to the attack of any unscrupulous person, and that, although innocent, she would, in the event of an attack, be convicted and still further degraded.

"In this first declaration, we wish only to make plain our view that the condition of things above revealed is intolerable."

*****

Printed in the United States
221185BV00004B/6/P

9 780955 705038